"If ever there was a need for help in pastoral visitation, it is now as we reel from the severe impact of Covid-19 on pastors, which has accelerated the decline of this vital pastoral practice. While older parishioners lament its demise, young pastors admit that they are at a loss about its true character and spiritual purpose. Some members of a congregation even dread a visit from their pastor because they regard it with suspicion, often rightly, as an exercise in surveillance and manipulation. This excellent pastoral handbook by Tyler Arnold is therefore most timely in its winsome, practical approach to this fraught issue. It is also most helpful in grounding pastoral visitations on the ministry of Jesus and the apostles and promoting their purpose to bring Jesus to people personally, each in their own situation, by listening to them to discern what is on their hearts, praying for them in keeping with what they have heard, and blessing them there wherever they may be on their journey through life. Oh, how I wish I had something like this when I began to work as a pastor!"

—John W. Kleinig,
emeritus lecturer, Australian Lutheran College,
Adelaide; author *Wonderfully Made:
A Protestant Theology of the Body*

"When I was a seminarian, our seminary president, Rev. Dr. Robert D. Preus used to say, 'If your people see you in their living rooms and in their pulpits, you'll never have any problems.' Of course, there are exceptions, but the truism is true. Over the decades, whenever I have encountered a pastor who's having a tough go in a congregation, often a young pastor, along with getting the issue of potential clinical depression, I inquire about visitation: 'Are you visiting your members? Have you tried to visit them in their homes? Have you gone to their businesses? Are you regularly getting to the shut-ins?' Of course, there are various arrangements in larger churches, but in most congregations these duties belong to the pastor. Invariably, the answer is 'No, not really.' Pastor Arnold wisely demonstrates that visitation is not only needed, it is also thoroughly biblical. The LORD visited his people of old in the prophets. The LORD visited through the ministry of the apostles in the New Testament. The greatest visitation is that of the incarnate Lord himself. A pastor is a visitor. There is no other way to be a curate of souls. Thank you, Pastor Arnold, for giving us the tools to share the blessed gospel of Jesus Christ, for the forgiveness of sins and great benefit and consolation of God's people."

—Matthew C. Harrison,
assistant pastor, Village Lutheran,
Ladue, Missouri;
president, The Lutheran Church Missouri Synod

"To pastors who are convinced that the deepest meaning in ministry revolves around building celebrated online platforms to which followers will inevitably flock, I want to hand this sensible little book. Tyler Arnold reminds readers that really good parish pastors root their ministry in proximity not platform. They understand the care of souls as up-close work that's primary not secondary to their calling."

—Peter W. Marty,
editor and publisher, *Christian Century*

Pastoral Visitation

For the Care of Souls

LEXHAM MINISTRY GUIDES

Pastoral Visitation

For the Care of Souls

TYLER C. ARNOLD

General Editor
Harold L. Senkbeil

LEXHAM PRESS

Pastoral Visitation: For the Care of Souls
Lexham Ministry Guides, edited by Harold L. Senkbeil

Copyright 2022 Tyler C. Arnold

Lexham Press, 1313 Commercial St., Bellingham, WA 98225
LexhamPress.com

Print ISBN 9781683596233
Digital ISBN 9781683596240
Library of Congress Control Number 2022933801

Lexham Editorial: Todd Hains, Kara Roberts, Jessi Strong, Mandi Newell
Cover Design: Joshua Hunt, Brittany Schrock
Typesetting: Fanny Palacios, Abigail Stocker

23 24 25 26 27 28 29 / IN / 12 11 10 9 8 7 6 5 4 3 2

*To all those whom God has blessed me
to serve in the parish.*

Contents

Part 1: Pastoral Foundations

Part 2: Pastoral Resources

Acts 20:28

Pay careful attention to yourselves and
to all the flock, in which the Holy Spirit
has made you overseers, to care
for the church of God,
which he obtained
with his own
blood.

Series Preface

Wʜᴀᴛ's ᴏʟᴅ ɪs ɴᴇw ᴀɢᴀɪɴ.

The church in ages past has focused her mission through every changing era on one unchanging, Spirit-given task: the care of souls in Jesus' name. Christian clergy in every generation have devoted themselves to bringing Christ's gifts of forgiveness, life, and salvation to people by first bringing them to faith and then keeping them in the faith all life long.

These people—these blood-bought souls—are cared for just as a doctor cares for bodies. The first step is carefully observing the symptoms of distress, then diagnosing the ailment behind these symptoms. Only after careful observation and informed diagnosis can a physician of souls proceed—treating not the symptoms, but the underlying disease.

Attention and intention are essential for quality pastoral care. Pastors first attentively listen with Christ's ears and then intentionally speak with Christ's mouth. Soul care is a ministry of the Word; it is rooted in the conviction that God's word is efficacious—it does what it says (Isa 55:10–11).

This careful, care-filled pastoral work is more art than science. It's the practical wisdom of theology, rooted in focused study of God's word and informed by the example of generations past. It's an aptitude more than a skillset, developed through years of ministry experience and ongoing conversation with colleagues.

The challenges of our turbulent era are driving conscientious evangelists and pastors to return to the soul care tradition to find effective tools for contemporary ministry. (I describe this in depth in my book *The Care of Souls: Cultivating a Pastor's Heart.*) It's this collegial conversation that each author in this series engages—speaking from their own knowledge and experience. We want to learn from each other's insights to enrich the soul care tradition. How can we best address contemporary challenges with the timeless treasures of the Word of God?

IN THE LEXHAM MINISTRY GUIDES YOU WILL meet new colleagues to enlarge and enrich your unique ministry to better serve the Savior's sheep and lambs with confidence. These men and women are in touch with people in different subcultures and settings, where they are daily engaged in learning the practical wisdom of the care of souls in real-life ministry settings just like yours. They will share their own personal insights and approaches to one of the myriad aspects of contemporary ministry.

Though their methods vary, they flow from one common conviction: all pastoral work is rooted in a pastoral habitus, or disposition. What every pastor does day after day is an expression of who the pastor is as a servant of Christ and a steward of God's mysteries (1 Cor 4:1).

Although the authors may come from theological traditions different than yours, you will find a wealth of strategies and tactics for practical ministry you can apply, informed by your own confession of the faith once delivered to the saints (Jude 1:3).

OUR LORD DOESN'T CALL US TO SUCCESS, AS IF the results were up to us: "Neither he who plants nor he who waters is anything, but only God who gives the growth" (1 Cor 3:7). No, our Lord asks us to be faithful laborers in the service of souls he has purchased with his own blood (Acts 20:28).

Nor does our Lord expect us to have all the answers: "I will give you a mouth and wisdom" (Luke 21:15). Jesus, the eternal Word of the Father, is the Answer who gives us words when we need them to give to our neighbors when they need them. After all, Jesus sees deeper into our hearts than we do; he knows what we need. He is the Wisdom of God in every generation (1 Cor 1:24).

But wisdom takes time. The Lord our God creates, redeems, and sanctifies merely by his words. He could give us success and answers now, but he usually doesn't. We learn over time through challenges and frustrations—even Jesus grew over time (Luke 2:52). The Lexham Ministry Guides offer practical wisdom for the church.

MY PRAYER IS THAT YOU GROW IN HUMBLE appreciation of the rare honor and responsibility that Christ Jesus bestowed on you in the power and presence of his Spirit: "As the Father has sent me, even so I am sending you" (John 20:21).

Father in heaven, as in every generation you send forth laborers to do your work and equip them by your word, so we pray that in this our time you will continue to send forth your Spirit by that word. Equip your servants with everything good that they may do your will, working in them that which is well pleasing in your sight. Through Jesus Christ our Lord. Amen.

Harold L. Senkbeil, General Editor
September 14, 2020
Holy Cross Day

Prayer for Visitors

GOD IMPLORES ALL OF HIS SERVANTS TO COME before him in prayer. The prayer below is designed for visitors who are about to embark on the task of caring for souls wherever they may be. This prayer could be used with other visitors or with those who are being visited. This prayer could also be used individually—the visitor speaking and responding with both parts.

In the name of the Father, Son, and Holy Spirit.
Amen.

O Lord, open my lips,
And my mouth will declare your praise. *Ps 51:15*
Let me dwell in your tent forever!
**Let me take refuge under the shelter
of your wings!** *Ps 61:4*
Blessed be the Lord God of Israel,
**For he has visited and redeemed
his people.** *Luke 1:68*

Let us pray.

That God would visit this place and drive far
from it all the snares of the enemy by sending his holy angels to protect and keep in
peace all those who dwell here.

That God would bless all within this dwelling
place with his peace, which surpasses all
understanding in every trial or temptation.

That God would grant strength to sustain those
being visited in his abundant grace.

Lord, in your mercy,
Hear our prayer.

That God would protect all visitors as they seek
to share the gospel to the lowly, the despised,
the broken-hearted, and the lost.

That God would procure a calm heart and a
sustained spirit when trials and tribulations
become unbearable within those who are
visited.

That God would grant visitors perseverance and
courage to speak the truth in love so that his
kingdom may be blessed through the blessings of truth, hope, and salvation.

Lord, in your mercy,
Hear our prayer.

Our Father who art in heaven
Hallowed be thy name,
Thy kingdom come,
Thy will be done on earth as it is in heaven;
Give us this day our daily bread;
And forgive us our trespasses as we forgive
    those who trespass against us;
And lead us not into temptation,
But deliver us from evil.
For thine is the kingdom and the power, and
    the glory forever and ever.
Amen.   *Matt 6:9–13*

Almighty God and Father, you promise your Holy
Spirit to every visitor that enters every home, hospital room, or institution.

Grant us comfort and strength as we carry out the
ministry of bearing up your message of hope and
salvation to your precious ones.

Guide and lead us as we share your word of law
to those who are confident in their sins and your
word of gospel to salve the wounds of the afflicted.

Grant your visitors faithful courage to proclaim your truth so that they may know your boundless love, through Jesus Christ, your Son, our Lord, who lives and reigns with you and the Holy Spirit one God, now and forever.

Amen.

The Lord almighty direct our days and our deeds in his peace.

Amen.

Preface

"A home-going pastor makes for
a church-going people."

THIS WELL-KNOWN ADAGE CANNOT BE QUAN-
tified, but it most certainly makes sense. Pastors
build relationships through visitation. Pastors
are blessed to get to know the needs of their
people better through visitation. Pastors actively
demonstrate God's love and care as they bring
the gospel comfort to where the sick convalesce,
the broken-hearted reside, and the lost build
their temples apart from God's house.

Being a home-going pastor is hard work. Quite
frankly, visitation can be one of the pastor's most
unpleasant tasks. It's time consuming. It's a hassle
trying to make appointments or finding people at
home. This age of cell phones and social media has
created new ways of communication that avoid
the intimacy of face-to-face contact. When visitation does occur, parishioners have been known to

use their private audience as a complaint session against the church and others. These challenges mixed together make for quite a distasteful recipe for ministry.

Yet, visitation is more than just one of many tasks for the pastor. Visitation is rather intimately connected and wrapped up in the very identity of the pastoral office. The pastor is a visitor who brings Jesus to the home and hospital room. The individual care of souls oftentimes relies on pastors moving toward those in need—toward the hospital, the care facility, or home. Just like a physician first gets to know the sick person and their illness before prescribing an appropriate course of treatment, the physician of the soul searches for the person's condition and adjusts divine medication accordingly.

First and foremost, this book is about pastoral care that moves from the Sunday morning altar toward God's people whenever and wherever the need occurs. The goal is to encourage pastors to reclaim something that has become antiquated (in the eyes of some) and more difficult to accomplish in our closed-off world today—that is, to reclaim the care of souls that moves into proximity of others by addressing spiritual needs and providing treatment for those who are despairing. For that reason, this book seeks to take the "how-to" of visitation to a deeper level. Not only does it address practical matters in a contemporary context, but it also delves into specific maladies visitors can expect to encounter.

Chapter 1 roots us into the visitation ministry of Jesus and builds a foundation from where all individual care resides—the proper application of the law and gospel to needful souls. Chapter 2 explores the pastor's identity as a visitor and touches on challenges pastors face along with a word of encouragement amid adversity. Chapter 3 considers the importance of how God connects to needs through the liturgy of the visit, which includes the pastor's work of listening to both God and the individual. Chapter 4 begins the practical application portion of the book by illustrating what to consider before and during visitation. Chapter 5 explores alternative means of contact beyond the pastoral visitation face-to-face contact including the training of lay visitors. Chapter 6 delves into five unique visitation scenarios where the specifics of individual pastoral care are addressed.

The way we visit has changed throughout the ages. But the necessity of it never will. With this short book, which complements Harold L. Senkbeil's *The Care of Souls: Cultivating a Pastor's Heart,* I hope to demonstrate the spiritual urgency for pastors to return to this classic method of individual soul care. Together, we will take a journey through the joys and the hardships of pastoral visitation. So, do come along with me, won't you?

Tyler C. Arnold
Palm Sunday, 2021

Part I

Pastoral Foundations

Chapter 1

God's Visitation:
Jesus at the Center

I LIVE IN A PARSONAGE NEXT TO THE CHURCH.
Church members and members of the community
know right where to find me.

I guess you could say this is a blessing and a
challenge.

At times, it's a challenge because strangers
have knocked on my door at all hours of the
night, asking for some sort of assistance, waking
my family and me in fear. Fortunately, these situations are few and far between.

It's a blessing that others know where I live
when members of the church or the community desire to bless our family. For example, one
member knocks on my door a couple of times a
year. With him are bags of Swiss chard from his
garden. He knows how my family enjoys eating

this green, leafy vegetable. Another member stops by and brings a jar of jalapeño peppers along with a couple of cucumbers for the family. Yet another time, the doorbell rings, and there on my porch is a member of our church, a man who serves on our properties committee, just dropping by, making sure everything is working the way it should in the house. It's the church's house, but his concern is not so much with the physical structure as it is with the people who live there.

Each of these visitors brought something valuable with them. No, I'm not talking about chard, peppers, or an inquiry as to how the parsonage is holding up. They brought the fruit of their labors. They brought a kind gesture. With them came a Christ-like concern for their neighbor who also happens to be their pastor.

As pastor, I'm the resident visitor, yet time after time I find myself on the receiving end of God's blessings through those I serve. They live out what God has called them to be—intimately identifying with the Savior that they act the way he acts. The incarnation shows us what visitation is: God's care through means for the sake of others. Visitors embody Christ as they bring all of his gracious blessings directly to individuals and communities.

God's word shows us how this happens. As in the Old Testament, the New Testament shows that there is a dual purpose for God's visitation: earthly and heavenly. The person and work of Jesus helps us to learn most of what we need to know about pastoral visitation.

THE PROMISE TO COME

In the Old Testament, there are many examples of how God visited his people to take care of their bodily needs. The Hebrew word *paqad* occurs 304 times, and most prominently means "to take an interest in a person."[1] In many English translations, this word is translated "to visit" within its appropriate setting. For example, God visits and gives food to famished Naomi and her daughters-in-law (Ruth 1:6). Their starving bellies needed God's gracious attention and he provided for them by visiting the earth, enriching it, and preparing it to provide grain (Ps 65:9). He enters this narrative through creation and delivers the appropriate and much needed blessing.

God takes a personal interest in our physical needs. He comes to provide aid for body and life. At the end of Genesis, Joseph promises his brothers that God will visit them and bring them out of

Egypt back to the land promised to Abraham (Gen 50:24). Four hundred years later, the enslaved Israelites saw how God, who saw their affliction, visited the people through his servant Moses. God himself came to bring them relief and freedom (Exod 4:31). God attaches his presence with the satisfaction of needs. God is not distant like some human king in his high court; rather, God gives relief by addressing our need through his presence. He satisfies our need and gives appropriate provision. Physical necessities are just the beginning of what God provides when he visits his creation.

The Lord visits Sarah and gives her an exceptional and remarkable promise. This gift is both a physical blessing for Sarah, the gift of a child, and a redeeming blessing for the world. "The LORD visited Sarah as he had said, and the LORD did to Sarah as he had promised" (Gen 21:1). God's favor turns toward Sarah and Abraham with a promise fulfilled—one that will eventually see its culmination in Jesus, the incarnate Lord. God provides both a physical son for Sarah and, from this son, the promised redeemer for the world.

There is something very special about the nature of God's promise of a redeemer. He chose to come and be with us in the flesh, born of a woman.

He chose the most humiliating way to bestow the most precious gift ever known—forgiveness by death on a cross. God determined that the only way to completely fulfill his promise was to come as close to us as possible. The embodiment of God in the flesh through the incarnation put the divine in our shoes. He experiences all of our joys and sorrows, our happy moments and our sufferings in close proximity to his creation. God's visitation is at the heart of the way he provides the renewal of our lives.

The Promise Revealed

Before Jesus was born, the aged priest Zechariah cried out what God in the flesh came to do: to visit his people and redeem them (Luke 1:68). God desires to come near those he loves and that's how he chose to deliver his intended gifts. This is the core of the gospel ministry: Jesus's presence in our presence. Each moment of Jesus's earthly ministry was God's personal encounter with his people. The incarnation demonstrates the very essence of how we understand God's visitation for us and our visitation toward each other.

A large part of Jesus's ministry was individual, face-to-face interactions. However, all of his ministry was visitation. There were different ways and reasons Jesus interacted with the people—it was not one-size-fits-all. God came near to listen to their needs. He came in close proximity to share an appropriate word of instruction or encouragement. Most of all, Jesus came near to offer his gifts of redemption to a condemned world. No matter the exact need, no matter how his visitation took place, every encounter was all about God in our midst.

Nicodemus visits with Jesus in the cover of darkness. He knows Jesus is a man who comes from God because of the signs and wonders he witnessed. Jesus uses this individual encounter to teach him what it means to be a faithful follower of Christ. "Truly, truly, I say to you, unless one is born of water and the Spirit, he cannot enter the kingdom of God" (John 3:5). The Pharisee doesn't understand what Jesus is saying. Jesus explains that no one can enter the kingdom of God without being reborn of water and the Spirit. The great tradition of the church has understood this to be about baptism—an encounter of water combined with God's word to grant the gift of true life and forgiveness. Jesus teaches Nicodemus that faith is not based on the awesome things one sees, but on God's presence in our lives.

Consider also the Samaritan woman in John 4. She didn't seem to be suffering from anything physical, but she was misguided in her understanding of God. When Jesus asks her to give him a drink, she was confused about why he, a Jew, would ask such a socially irresponsible thing from a Samaritan woman. Jesus encounters this woman not to make an example of her negatively, but to show her (and his disciples) an important reality about himself—that he is the living water for eternal life. If she can drink this life, if Jesus IS the living water, then her eternal life is directly dependent upon her Lord coming near to her and actively giving himself to her. He comes near her.

When Jesus visits Capernaum in Galilee, an official asks Jesus to heal his ill son (John 4:46–54). Jesus's ministry is not about signs and wonders, it's about the substance of what Jesus comes to give. The official does not come before Jesus that day because he saw signs and wonders. He has a living faith. He believes that Jesus can heal his son because this carpenter's son from Nazareth is who he is—the Son of God. "Sir, come down before my child dies" (John 4:49). The official wanted the Savior to come near the ill child to heal him. It makes sense to assume that healing requires being near the ill person. In other words, he must come near the sickness to rid the boy of it. Yet Jesus heals the boy by his word—the official believed the word Jesus spoke (John 4:50). And though Jesus did not directly visit the boy, he did encounter faith and honored the request of the man who had this faith by healing his Son.

The encounter between Jesus and the Centurion in Matthew 8:5–10 is another example of the healing presence of Jesus in the lives of the faithful. While Jesus healed the gentile's servant from a distance, his first words to this leader of one hundred soldiers were, "I will come and heal him" (Matt 8:7). The Centurion knew that Jews do not usually enter the homes of gentiles, so he requested that Jesus do what needed to be done at a distance—which, of course, he did.

Jesus honors two requests from the man who has a greater faith than anyone Jesus has found in Israel (Matt 8:10). The first, "Just say the word," was a request made from unworthiness to having Jesus come near his home. The second, to heal his "unworthy" servant. Jesus stood face-to-face with an unworthy man who demonstrated a personal faith that knew Jesus only had to speak his healing balm.

Sometimes Jesus visits a region or a town where he is sought out by someone who has some sort of need or concern. Other times, Jesus is doing the seeking. He's the one who comes right alongside the person in need and offers his help.

There was a pool in Jerusalem called Bethesda, where people with every kind of disability or disease would gather. It was a popular spot. It was believed that this pool had healing powers. When this pool bubbled up, angels from heaven were supposed to have stirred the waters.

At this pool, Jesus finds a man described as an "invalid for thirty-eight years" (John 5:5). Jesus knew that the man had been there a long time. And so, he asks a question meant to grab the man's attention: "Do you want to be healed?" (John 5:6). The man doesn't give the obvious answer. Instead, he says why he thinks he can't be healed: "I have no one to put me into the pool when the water is stirred up" (John 5:7).

Jesus knew that true healing did not come from popular Greek religious beliefs—a pool thought to be stirred up by heavenly hosts. No, this healing comes by word and faith. The Word made flesh stood in the presence of the man, having with it the power to make him physically whole. The man trusted, in faith, that Jesus's words would allow him to experience the miraculous. He believed that this Word that had come near to him, that met him right where he lay, had the power to heal. In both this story and the next, Jesus's presence is accompanied by his restoring power wherever he goes and whenever that happens to be.

Jesus's healing not only addresses physical ailments, but also treats disordered thinking regarding morality. In Galilee, Jesus confronts the Pharisees with a simple question: "Which one of you who has a sheep, if it falls into a pit on the Sabbath, will not take hold of it and lift it out?" (Matt 12:11). Jesus asks this rhetorical question to which everyone must say yes. So why would they not also rescue a man? Then Jesus presents a man at the synagogue with a paralyzed hand and shows how doing good for others on the Sabbath takes priority over the too-strict application of the law. More so, Jesus asserts that God never intended this strict application of the law; it had morphed into a gross misunderstanding of how the Sabbath is kept holy.

Again, Jesus comes near to teach and to heal. He breaks through the barrier of misinterpretation by illustrating a real-life example of God's will and compassion to a mixed-up group of self-righteous devotees. Closeness gave Jesus the ability to be understood, to make himself as clear as possible, and to say and do exactly what he intended. There was no question who healed the man's hand or what good a person is allowed to do on the Sabbath. Nearness brings what may be blurry from a distance into focus.

Jesus, once again, weds teaching with healing in the account of the man born blind in John 9. The disciples want to learn from Jesus about fault and blame. Together, they encounter the perfect example: a blind man they meet as they simply pass along the way. "Rabbi, who sinned, this man or his parents, that he was born blind?" (John 9:2). The disciples thought this was the perfect opportunity to learn about the effects of sin since, according to beliefs at the time, someone had to do something wrong for this man to be this way.

Jesus, however, counters the question by giving quite an unexpected answer and by healing the man in a most extraordinary way. Jesus answers the disciples with a third option to their question. It wasn't the sin of the man or his parents, but rather it was so that God could display good works for the benefit of the kingdom through him. Instead of affirming one of the two negatives, Jesus shows the positive use God intends through this blindness.

Jesus heals the man of blindness by mixing mud with his own spit. In Jesus's time, people thought human saliva carried medicinal properties and, for this reason, may have been used to show how Jesus *is* the medicine that brings light to the eyes of the blind.

However, Jesus potentially violates yet another rabbinic rule concerning the Sabbath: the kneading of dough is among the thirty-nine forms of work forbidden and mixing earth with saliva was thought to be covered in that rule. But just like the man with a withered hand, Jesus shows that service pleasing to God is service not to be avoided. And Jesus comes so near to the blind man that he touches him. His healing touch brings light to the one in darkness. Just as one must receive the medicine to experience the effect, Jesus must come near, visit, and redeem with his life-giving touch through his appointed means.

Jesus's visitations often appear unexpected, unwelcomed, and unethical. Perhaps no more excellent example of this is offered in the holy Scriptures than when he breaks all social and ceremonial barriers by touching and healing a man with leprosy.

In Matthew 8, we are told that great crowds followed him, and, within this setting, a leper somehow finds his way to the feet of Jesus. We might think this man did all the hard work. He avoided detection, he discovered Jesus, and he mustered the courage to speak in faith, "Lord, if you will, you can make me clean" (Matt 8:2).

And then the remarkable happened. Jesus did not rebuke him for being amid the crowds when the law of Moses required that he live apart from the community of Israel (Mark 1:40–45). He did not just answer his request by simply speaking this wellness into existence. No, Jesus made him whole by literally touching the afflicted man. By every societal and ceremonial standard, Jesus would become unclean by touching such a man.

But the opposite happened. Jesus delivered his cleanness to the unclean man instead of receiving the leper's uncleanliness. The Savior's blessed touch, when in close proximity to this diseased man, made the broken child of God whole. By Jesus touching the man, he demonstrates to us that

God comes near, reaches out, and places his healing hand upon sinners—no matter how marred by affliction and uncleanliness.

Jesus is not only the primary example of visitation ministry, but the very embodiment of what that ministry includes. Jesus defines the activity of ministers. Jesus's life not only includes but incorporates a ministry of presence. His activity of sharing instruction, comfort, and healing was not just a part of the life and times of the Savior, but rather the very reason for his incarnation.

Jesus came to be with people in order to save humanity. He chose the way to accomplish this activity. He came to be like us in every way except without sin—to put on flesh and blood and live among his people. If God so desired, he could have planned out a different, less interactive way. He could have pronounced some holy dictum from heaven and never entered our humanity. Think of it: he could have safely tucked himself away, never to encounter his tarnished creation. But he didn't.

So, as a result, his living and caring for us is our living and caring for each other. He tells us, "For I was hungry and you gave me food, I was thirsty and you gave me drink, I was a stranger and you welcomed me" (Matt 25:35). Jesus was not these things. However, our neighbor might be. Jesus explains that service to one another is service to the Lord. Since his service was to us directly, we directly serve our neighbor. And no greater service was that of Jesus on the cross. Only through a God who would truly come and visit his people—even in the most intimate, sorrowful, and personal way of death—is this accomplished. Now, we too are given this role. It belongs to Jesus, which means that now it belongs to us.

CHAPTER 2

The Pastor's Visitation: God's Work as Identity

Iago's mysterious and deceitful character in Shakespeare's *Othello* bewilders Roderigo by speaking about himself, "I am not what I am." Iago, Othello's primary antagonist, constantly plays a game of deception by keeping others guessing about reality. His intent is to show that he is not what he appears to be. He is in disguise and playing a role. Everyone is left to wonder if they can trust their own judgement. Iago gives the illusion of a false reality. He deceives by identifying as something he is not.

Contrast Iago's confusing and deceptive identity with the way the Lord identifies himself in the book of Exodus. Moses asks God what he should say to the children of Israel if they ask him the

Lord's name. The Lord tells Moses, "Say this to the people of Israel, 'I AM has sent me to you' " (Exod 3:14).

The Lord's name comprises his identity. He is, "I AM"—the one who exists for the benefit of his people. When they were in slavery, the Egyptians had different names for deities. The names for these deities presupposed God's nature and operations, and that God would manifest through deeds the nature expressed in his name. Naturally, the Israelites wanted to know God's name so they could know how he would manifest his deeds for them.

The name that Christians associate most closely with the name of God is "Jesus Christ." His name means "He Saves," and Christ, his office, means, "The anointed one." His name and the description of who he is before God and humankind clearly articulate God's good intentions. His name is much more than just something that describes who he is. This name embodies God's accomplishment for humankind. It defines not only his character but the reason for the incarnation in the first place. "He Saves" is not some cutesy label that Mary and Joseph wanted for this special child. His name was pre-ordained and given to define God's essence— The Savior of the World.

Christian pastors not only associate with the name of Jesus, they intimately identify with it. Of course, as Christians, we are named as people who believe that Jesus is our Savior. But we are more than that. Christians embody Christ Jesus through our faith, words, and deeds. Pastors, specifically, are called to a particular task within the congregation for the sake of the community in a particular place with specific responsibilities. Pastors publicly preach God's word, administer the sacraments of the church, and lead the Divine Service. (Worship is sometimes called Divine Service because God, the Divine, serves his people in worship.)

Though the pastor is obviously not Jesus, he does represent and stand in the place of Christ. He speaks the word of God as if God himself is speaking to his people. When the pastor speaks words of forgiveness to repentant sinners, he is not speaking for himself, but for God. This is what God calls the pastor to do.

THE PASTOR AS UNDER-SHEPHERD

In the New Testament, shepherds identify with the company they keep—sheep. Shepherds are the leaders of the sheep. Their well-being depends on the care of the shepherd. The sheep need good grazing ground, and the shepherd has the distinct responsibility of leading the sheep to nourishing places to eat. If the shepherd does not lead the sheep to green pastures (Ps 23), the sheep will eventually starve.

Shepherds must also defend the sheep. Predators are always looking for ways to elude the shepherd's view and catch an unsuspecting sheep off-guard—perhaps one that wandered too far from the herd. The shepherd put his life on the line to protect the sheep because they are not simply property. The sheep are the shepherd's livelihood, an extension of the self—his identity. A shepherd without sheep is not a shepherd at all. The sheep that he keeps makes him who he is.

The name "pastor" is a fitting title for those called into the office of the holy ministry since the name means shepherd. Specifically, pastors are under-shepherds of the Good Shepherd—Jesus. The title of shepherd is more than just descriptive of a pastor's duties; it's prescriptive of who he is. Under-shepherds embody Jesus's love and care by being the instrument of mercy that brings care and protection to the sheep. Jesus places pastors amid the flock because there is no better place for them to get to know vital needs and to watch out for predators lurking in the darkness. They desire to come near the sheep at the most opportune time to attack and devour. The shepherd may have no idea when this might be. So, the shepherd must remain near to guard the sheep with a vigilant eye. His proximity to the sheep is essential since their safety depends on it.

THE PASTOR AS OVERSEER

The first time I read 1 Timothy in Greek, I balked. Not because of the overseer's qualifications—"above reproach, the husband of one wife, sober-minded, self-controlled, respectable, hospitable, able to teach," and so on (1 Tim 3:2). Rather, what struck me as strange is the English translation of the word *episkopē*. As I got to know this word better, the better I understood what it really means.

At first glance, "overseer" didn't seem like the right word to describe a pastor. It seemed too dictatorial and hands-off. I pictured a man sitting high above a group of workers watching their every move. This man's job was to observe the hard labor while barking out orders to the workers below. His only job was to check the laborers' progress and tell them what needed to be done next.

Perhaps I got this imagery from my father, a hard-working craftsman who worked most of his adult life for the telephone company. He told me stories about how the project foreman stopped by in his shiny truck to make sure my dad and his co-workers were doing their job and making sufficient progress. My dad told me that he wore a hardhat every day because work on the top of telephone poles is dangerous. The foreman never wore a hardhat. There was no need. He'd be back in his truck and off to the next job site in no time. The boss, the foreman, *the overseer* remained sufficiently removed from the dangerous labor.

The overseer described in the New Testament is not a foreman who stands at a distance away from danger, but a pastor who comes near to visit.

First and foremost, the office of overseer is one that exemplifies God's interest in others. God demonstrated this by caring for the physical needs of his people and by promising the coming Messiah. God's interest in his people relieved their needs by putting what was vital for their sake right in front of them. He provided for their needs by coming into contact with his people with relief. The person in the office takes an interest in the needs of those he serves by coming into contact and addressing the need.

Second, the verb form of *episkopē* is *episkopeo* which means, "to visit." The very definition of the noun "overseer" embodies the active meaning of the verb. The overseer *is* a visitor who takes an interest in those God gives to serve.

Pastors are visitors. And visitation isn't just one of their many external tasks. The pastor's essential function cannot be separated from the primary meaning of who the pastor is. The pastoral office, in essence, embodies the activity of visitation. They are one and the same in function and essence.

Pastors shepherd God's flock. They watch for ravenous wolves, false doctrine, or anything that can harm God's flock. God charges pastors with the task of rebuking the wayward sheep and speaking the law to those who remain comfortable in their sins. Also, the pastor must understand the condition of the soul, identify spiritual needs, and comfort the weary with the gospel.

Although sin is the common denominator of all spiritual distress, symptoms manifest themselves differently in each individual. Pastors must get to know these needs by getting to know the ones they care for in order to prescribe the appropriate remedy according to God's word. St. John

Chrysostom famously asserted that pastors need a thousand eyes to observe every habit of the soul.

Considering all that pastors are given to do, it's an understatement to say that the pastor's call to care for God's flock is a challenging one. There is no possible way he can fulfill his divinely appointed and interpersonal vocation from any other location than right where the sheep happen to be. The essence of the pastoral office has a "with" identity. From Jesus to the apostles, the New Testament church clearly articulates visitation as a primary pattern of pastoral care. The essence and function of the office go hand in hand.

Apostolic Ministry and Pastoral Visitation

Jesus's ministry took place in a variety of settings where he was intentionally present in order to address individual needs. The apostles carried out this type of one-on-one ministry in the New Testament church by visiting "from house to house" (Acts 5:42). Their visits had an important purpose—to preach and teach Jesus as the Christ. The gospel was boldly professed in the face of danger in the homes of those who needed to hear. St. Paul courageously does the same when he recalls how he did not shrink from declaring anything publicly or from house to house (Acts 20:20).

Paul and the other apostles carried out Christ-like ministry by not only modeling the behavior of Jesus but also by bringing Jesus to where the people are. Paul went from town to town, met the people in houses and synagogues, and proclaimed the essence of life. His ministry of presence brought more than just words of comfort, but also the powerful salve of the gospel word that enacted God's righteousness right into the very lives of individuals. Pastors, in turn, model this type of ministry behavior and are also the very instruments by which God delivers forgiveness and life. The apostolic examples of visitation reflect much of what pastors still struggle with today.

Visitation Challenges

Pastors are God's servants, called to bring the good news to the nations in every place and in every time. This world, however, is defiant of the gospel. Sinners want what their itching ears want to hear. Our flawed world fills our hearts and minds with the lie that God is not present or doesn't care for his people. Therefore, the pastor's vocation to preach and baptize is frequently beset with hardships. This is evident in the ministry of the apostles as well.

Paul's missionary visitations to the wayward souls in Lystra, Iconium, and Antioch (Acts 14) led him right into extreme resistance and bodily harm. He fled for his life from Iconium and was stoned nearly to death at Lystra. For Paul, the bold proclamation of the gospel constantly put his livelihood in jeopardy. Amazingly, Paul went back to share the gospel with them more than once. Pastors today, at least domestically and for the most part, are not putting life and limb on the line like Paul. We know that for some brave missionaries who serve abroad, the threat of bodily harm is a reality. Yet, regardless of personal safety, visitation remains among the most distasteful and feared aspects of their work.

Visitation is time consuming. It is often difficult to justify the time spent making home visits compared to the perceived value and efficacy of those calls. Visitation can be most distasteful when the pastor is confronting specific misdeeds or transgressions face-to-face. Pastors face intense inner resistance toward risk-laden encounters when they minister on unfamiliar turf. Pastors feel much more comfortable addressing indiscretions from the pulpit. Congregants expect the pastor to do so anyway. Even the pastor's study is a more comfortable place since the individual or couple is taking the initiative to come and speak to the pastor. Here, there is at least a pre-conceived readiness to hear bad news if necessary.

The reformer of Strasbourg Martin Bucer could be alluding to Paul's troubled visitations in Acts 14 or any pastor in the modern age when he wrote, "There is no ministry more subject to ingratitude and rebellion than that of the care of souls."[2] Pastoral visitation or individual pastoral care is sometimes called "extraordinary soul care" because it extends beyond the ordinary care given and received in the Divine Service. Care through visitation is specifically tailored to address individual needs. Extraordinary soul care allows a conversation to occur—a forum for dialogue about concerns, hurts, desires, and despairs. Here is where the pastor can discover the symptoms of underlying spiritual problems, diagnose those problems, and address them according to God's word. For these important reasons, extraordinary care is not optional care but rather a vital extension of what the people receive from the pulpit and altar.

Years ago, Roger and Samantha, along with their children Kyle and Olivia, attended the church I serve. They slowly began to disengage from church friendships, stopped coming to activities, and eventually quit coming to church. As my concern for their spiritual well-being grew, I decided to call and make an appointment for a visit. I intentionally wanted to go to them instead of bringing them into my study. I wanted to be where they were most comfortable—on their turf. The sacred and familiar space of the family kitchen table or living room allows those receiving visitation to feel more relaxed and in control.

I was a little nervous, to be honest. I wasn't sure why they stopped coming to church. Was it something I said? Something I did? I knew the best way to discover the problem is to hear it directly from them. I already saw the symptoms of their troubles—separation from the community of believers. But now I wanted to discover the cause so I can begin addressing with them the main issue.

It turned out that their pre-teen child, Kyle, was having problems with another child at our church. The trouble began at school, carried over to Sunday school, and eventually got back to the parents. Each set of parents sided with their children and began to become at odds with each other in the process. At school, the administration got involved because there was an accusation of bullying. Both families were called into the principal's office, and matters just got worse. The hard feelings turned to anger, and Roger and Samantha stopped coming to church to avoid any further confrontation.

My goal was to accurately assess the situation by hearing the whole story from their perspective. I needed to attentively assess the matter holistically in order to discern the threat to their spiritual well-being and, subsequently, their faith. Only then could I accurately address the threat with the word of God. I needed to have one ear listening to the soul's distress while having the other ear listening to the voice of Jesus. Intentional treatment comes only from the word of God since only God can heal spiritual distress. Anger at the other family was the root cause of their disengagement from the community of believers and became a barrier to receiving God's nourishment in the Divine Service.

This type of extraordinary one-on-one soul care allowed me to diagnose the problem and apply an intentional treatment according to the word of God. But, that wasn't the end of it. This family still struggled to return to church. The other family—they were hurting and needed pastoral care as well—also began to fall away from the church slowly. Both families went their separate ways and joined different churches in the area. There was nothing I could do.

Dietrich Bonhoeffer once mentioned that every unsuccessful pastoral visit is a difficult judgment against us because it will display our lack of spiritual experience and power.[3] Humanly, we desire to quantify the quality of our visitation by the result rendered. We tend to forget that pastoral visitation is God's call to action with outcomes left up to God. St. Paul reminds us, "I planted, Apollos watered, but God gave the growth" (1 Cor 3:6). Pastors seek the opportunity to care for the flock; the result of that care belongs solely to God alone.

In Acts 14, Paul returned to the places where he was met with much resistance to strengthen and encourage the disciples. He implored them to continue in the faith and said that the way of the kingdom of God was through many tribulations. For whatever reason or wherever God's servants visit, problems occur. These problems are discouraging and many pastors think that visitation is futile and worthless. But make no mistake about it, there are excellent and indispensable reasons to carry forth the ministry of pastoral visitation. God's flock is dispersed and scattered vulnerably throughout a hazardous world. They need a pastor to care for their needs, shield them from predators, and lead them to clean water and nourishment. James reminds us, "Religion that is pure and undefiled before God the Father is this: to visit orphans and widows in their affliction" (Jas 1:27a).[4]

Visitation Encouragement

Paul told the newly appointed Ephesian elders (pastors) that they will endure the inevitable persecutions of imprisonment and affliction (Acts 20:18–35). At the end of the sermon, he encourages the elders to exercise their office in faithfulness and guard the sheep entrusted to them. He says, "And now I commend you to God and to the word of his grace, which is able to build you up and to give you the inheritance among all those who are sanctified" (Acts 20:32). The elders in Ephesus will need the Lord's power and strength to carry out their duties because troubles and persecution abound for ministers who bring God's word to a chaotic and disillusioned world.

Pastoral visitation always has an element of uncertainty. Attitudes and emotions are difficult to anticipate, even when parishioners are expecting their pastor at the door. Pastors may worry for any number of reasons: the potential of confrontation, ensuring confident responses, or feeling ill-equipped to handle someone's particular challenge are common concerns for pastors during visitation. Whatever the case, uncertainty about problematic issues, reactions, and fitting responses may trouble the pastor's heart.

Mike served on our church's board of directors and ushered a couple of months out of the year for Sunday morning services. He and his wife ran into marriage problems, and they eventually divorced. Besides the financial burdens of the breakup, Mike also lost primary custody of their three children. The breakup left him feeling lost and hopeless. And because his ex-wife's mother and father attended our church, he didn't feel comfortable at our church any longer. Even on the weekends he had the kids, Mike stopped coming to church.

Three times before the divorce, Mike and his wife came into my study to talk about their troubles. They didn't communicate anymore. He was never home for the kids. She was always nagging him. These were the common refrains shared with me each time we came together. We talked about communication, responsibility, and understanding. However, I did not feel equipped to walk with them through these challenges. So, I referred them to a licensed marriage counselor. Although they went to counseling faithfully for almost a year, the marriage still ended.

I saw his wife quite often—every Sunday, in fact. But Mike never came around. I knew why he didn't, and yet I did nothing. I knew he felt uncomfortable because of the divorce and because her parents go to our church. I understood this, so I just let him be. I figured I wouldn't feel comfortable either, so I would probably do the same thing. I knew in my heart of hearts that I should visit him, but I didn't. I finally called on him about a year later. I found out quickly this was a big mistake.

Mike was devastated that no one from the church tried to contact him and see how he was doing. He was crushed that his pastor never visited to help him sort out the tangled web that was his life and to encourage him to come back to church. This was a huge mistake on my part. I should have visited sooner. I should have asked about his emotional well-being and fostered the spiritual comfort he so desperately needed when he was at his lowest. He let me have it, shouting at me because the church and his pastor abandoned him at his most critical time. I deserved it. I never felt like such a failure in my calling as a pastor than at that very moment.

Pastors may not visit because they fear what kind of reception they will receive. Pastors tremble because parishioners may point out how they have neglected their duties in the realm of individual pastoral care—even when those they serve have neglected their duty as Christians by separating themselves from the body of Christ. Such circumstances expose the pastor's inadequacies and even cause shame because they have not carried out this important task.

We dare not forget we are human pastors addressing human needs. Though called to be above reproach, human pastors fall into human habits, much like those we serve. If that gap of closeness grows wider over time, our anxiety over what they might say if we were to call on them also grows.

One of the most challenging duties for a pastor is to deal intimately with people in personal relationships. Someone once asked Gregory of Nazianzus a most challenging question to which Gregory responded, "I would rather answer that one in the pulpit!"[5] It's easier to deal with difficult needs from the sacred enclosure of the pulpit than to face them alone in the intimate relationship of a pastoral visit. The pulpit acts as a kind of buffer between the pastor and the people. Church members expect a public discourse of exhortation within the setting of the Divine Service. The preacher addresses sin, calls for repentance, demands that Christians live as Christ intends, and no one retorts. At least not at that moment. But during intimate personal conversations, emotions can boil over into blame, and the pastor may be the target. Whether the outburst is justified or not, human pastors who address human hurts may fear this type of personal confrontation.

Yet, the ministry is active. It moves from God's delivery of word and sacrament in the church into the very homes of individuals and families. The ministry is not passive, waiting for people to join a Bible study or social group within the congregation.

The ministry of the pastor does not sit behind a desk and wait for members to make appointments in order to talk about what troubles their hurting hearts. It is true: at times, we must overcome our fears and deliver the important word straight to the doorstep. But we are never alone in either our encouragement or reproach. The Lord delivers and is present and active helping us move beyond our deep-seated fears. The prophet reminds us, "so shall my word be that goes out from my mouth; it shall not return to me empty, but it shall accomplish that which I purpose, and shall succeed in the thing for which I sent it" (Isa 55:11).

The pastor goes where the people are found. He must, as Ezekiel points out, "sit where they sit" and learn what the real needs are (Ezek 3:15). Hirelings, who are more concerned about self-interest than service, keep their distance and run from the problems (John 10:12). But true under-shepherds follow the example of the Good Shepherd, who always had time for individuals and never kept anyone on hold. As mentioned before, a shepherd must know his sheep, feed them, and seek out the lost (John 10:3, 4, 14, 16; Luke 15:4). As an overseer, he pays attention to himself and actively watches out for those under his care and visits them as the essence of his name suggests (Acts 20:28).

And yet, the pastor is described in the Scriptures as still even more. The pastor is a fisher who goes out to catch men (Matt 4:19). The pastor is a servant who must go wherever he can to reach outsiders and compel them to come in (Luke 14:23). All this requires personal effort and individual attention. For the shepherd, the overseer, the fisher, the servant—God's called ministers of the Word—visitation does not merely become a thing to do within ministry, but rather the means by which to accomplish the essence of what ministry entirely involves.

The spiritual needs of those we serve are best addressed quickly, not waiting for the hurting member to call the pastor and join him in his study. How blessed it is for the pastor to have the opportunity to speak directly concerning a specific sin and proclaim the medicine of life in the gospel when the crushed sinner knows not where to turn. Be heartened, beloved in the Lord, by the words of St. Paul that strengthen us to take courage and be where our people need us to be at the particular time of need, even when hindrances (whether they be our own short-comings, the parishioner's, or the world's) attempt to stand in our way.

The Lord teaches us that his ministers are simply to endeavor to lead to his church and to the perfect fellowship of his salvation all those who wish to come, no matter how wretched and corrupted they may be—indeed, not only to lead but to urge and compel them.[6] Whether it be the lapsed member or the new family that just moved in down the street, the pastor has the blessed opportunity to meet the spiritual needs of any person, at any place, with the knowledge that Jesus himself has commissioned his people into action for the sake of each of these needy souls.

Pastors are called to be God's foot soldiers in the cosmic battle against the principalities and evil powers of the universe. Armed with God's word, there is nothing that the visitor cannot handle because the visitor is never alone. Whether it be our ministry to the frail, the infirm, or the grossly delinquent, the writer of Hebrews reminds us of our Lord's promise: "I will never leave you nor forsake you" (Heb 13:5).[7] Those words ring true not only for those who receive the blessed ministry of Christ but also for those whom God uses as the givers. John Kleinig reminds us in his masterful book *Grace Upon Grace* that our holy calling involves a regular pilgrimage from Earth to heaven and then back again.[8] The Triune God accompanies ministers who bring the means of grace from the ordinary setting of the Sunday morning Divine Service out into homes and hospital rooms. God's liturgical movement toward individuals begins where the Lord promises to be found.

CHAPTER 3

God's Story in Our Story: Using Liturgy and Listening

ALL OF US HAVE A STORY. MY STORY BEGINS IN a small, working-class town in southwestern Illinois, outside of St. Louis. My father was a hard-working craftsman, and my mother, a faithful stay-at-home mom. They raised me in a Christian home where I was taught to love my Lord and my neighbor. We were active members of the Lutheran church where I grew up. We hardly ever missed a Sunday. I served as an acolyte most every Sunday during my teenage years. I led youth group, taught Vacation Bible School, and even made visits to prospective members. I learned the value of visitation by going with my mother to homes in the community, inviting children to Sunday school.

Here is where the story of my love for visitation begins. My story, who I am, what I love, and who loves me cannot be told apart from the church's story.

The church has a story, and Jesus is at the center. The life of Christ—his birth, life, death, and resurrection—is the foundation of the story of the Christian Church. We confess this story in our worship. Jesus Christ, crucified and risen, is present among us in the preaching of the gospel and the sacramental life of the church. To tell the world this blessed story, God gives his words and sacraments to show how his presence resides among us in his flesh, telling us the story of a world made new in him.

Worship gathers God's people together as he tells his story of redemption through his word and sacraments. God actively enters our world through the Spirit's power, and brings heaven to earth—life into death. For this reason, worship is much more than our response to God's grace. Rather, a true understanding of worship is to realize God's activity among his people. God actively gives his healing and grace, his comfort and forgiveness of sins.

Worship is sometimes called Divine Service because God, the Divine, serves his people in worship.

He gathers his guests around his life-giving word and precious sacraments and actively feeds them through these appointed means. Often, the Divine Service revolves around a *liturgy* that makes up the order in which worshipers carry out the service.

Today, when people hear the word liturgy, they may get the wrong impression. Some may exclusively think of the hymnal they use as "the liturgy." Others may believe that forms of worship inhibit the free expression of the Holy Spirit—they're too restrictive and therefore not beneficial. But the liturgy is much more than forms and ceremonies, which differ from one Christian tradition to the next. It first and foremost describes the theological content, namely, how God communicates his word. It is a normative structure of the word that tells the story of God's coming for the sake of redemption.

The use of forms and ceremonies serve an important purpose. They teach the people what they need to know about Christ. Liturgical order, then, is not merely an association of outward ties and rites but rather an association of faith and of the Holy Spirit in the human hearts. For this reason, liturgy also ties God's people together with a Christ-centered common order no matter where God meets his people—in church or the home.

This is especially important to the homebound who feel particularly separated from the church community. The liturgy's familiar words are the sweet sounds and gifts of Christian worship brought into the homes of those who are unable to join the gathering of believers on Sunday. Thus, the care of souls through visitation is liturgical in function.

The Liturgical Function of Visitation

I sat there with Carol at her dining room table. I unzipped the black canvas bag I routinely carry when I visit shut-ins and pulled out a small chalice, a tiny glass flask filled with wine, a container that held two hosts, and a small plate called a paten.

As I began to set up for Holy Communion like I had many times before, tears welled up in Carol's eyes. She knew that the sweet words of the gospel, prayers with her pastor, and jubilant hymns would soon fill her house. Worship was about to begin, and this was her blessed opportunity to stand in the presence of God. God, breaking forth into her world and coming to where Carol sat that day.

Though she was unable to attend church with her fellow worshipers, Carol was carried by God into the community of the faithful. She sang with the church, received God's gifts with the church, and communed with the church. Carol joined with the church from her home in the familiar liturgical responses known to her since childhood. Emotionally, it brought her to tears. She spoke to me joy-filled words through her soft, crackling voice: "Pastor, I miss church so much. It's always been such a big part of my life. Thank you for bringing church to my house."

Carol has a story—a heartbreaking and tragic story. Her son died of cancer while in his forties. Not long afterward, her husband passed away from complications resulting from an elective surgery. A year later, her other son died of a brain aneurism while driving home from work. She often described her life as disjointed and chaotic. Everything got turned upside down in a short amount of time. Her despair left her feeling helpless, alone, and abandoned. Carol longed for a sense of normalcy to come back to her life.

At that point in her life, worship in her home was the closest thing to normal that Carol had. The familiar order of service—God's word, psalms and hymns, the sermon, and Holy Communion— brought Carol into direct contact with the Divine. God himself served Carol though the liturgical context of the church. She was incorporated into the body of Christ, which is made up of members of both the community of the church and the celestial community of heaven.

There is a part of the Communion liturgy in the Divine Service called the Proper Preface that reminds participants that we come together "with the angels and archangels and all the company of heaven we laud and magnify your holy name and evermore praising you and saying: Holy, Holy, Holy Lord God of Sabaoth." One time, after we sang this part of the Communion liturgy, Carol said to me, "I love that part, Pastor. It reminds me that I'm a part of the church even here in my home and that this is the place that I'm closest to the angels, to heaven, to God, and my husband and sons." God places Carol within the more excellent story of redemption and eternal life.

Divine Service has a rhythm to it. God breaks into this dark world and brings the blessed gifts of eternal life. We respond to those gifs with thanksgiving and praise. The Lord enters our brokenness, our tragic stories, and shares his story of redemption with us. He comes to bring us into his story of undeserved grace by making his story our own. Jesus entered into this messy world of our making and was faithful unto death so that those who are dead in their sins might be restored and made whole in God's image.

Divine Service is the framework of pastoral care—a mutual and critical relationship between God and man. It informs pastoral care of the community and the history of God's journey to his people in the incarnation. Since God's story is the foundation for the care of souls and since soul care is the end goal for visitation, it is vital to incorporate God's story (through his word) into the story of those who are visited by him.

God Speaks to His People

Please, don't get me wrong. I'm not imposing a new law for pastoral visitation, but instead proposing a more excellent way of telling the story of Jesus for the life of all. The whole function of the church is the care of souls. The church's liturgy helps incorporate God's word of comfort into individual lives and serves as a bridge from the Sunday morning altar where God gives his gifts to the living room or kitchen table.

Visitors play the essential role by taking these gifts to homes and hospital rooms and performing these tasks when necessary. Visitors are God's instruments, blessed "letters from Christ" (2 Cor 3:3), for bringing his ordinary gifts found in the Divine Service into the extraordinary situations of personal life circumstances. What better words could possibily be shared with the needy, the brokenhearted, or the anxious than those that come directly from the Lord?

In visitation—as it always is—liturgy is a conversation between God and his people. God speaks, and humankind responds. Sunday morning preaching must not remain an isolated, mono-directional discourse. Rather, the purpose of Christian preaching is to enter into a conversation with God—God speaks, and we respond in word and deed. A conversation with God puts us in his presence. God is at hand where his word is pronounced. But because it is God with whom we converse, human answers are called prayers, praises, songs, and confessions.

The conversation enters the sphere of the liturgical—we speak what God speaks. His words are comfort and consolation on our lips. God's conversation with us, and our response in word and deed with God's own words is how God serves us through liturgy.

The liturgy is grounded in biblical content and bound directly to the service of God toward his people. It is fundamentally intertwined with the Divine Service. Therefore, liturgy can serve as a valuable instrument for the sharing of the gospel in the home or hospital room. A misconception about liturgy is that it's too formal and too impersonal. It only belongs to some faith traditions or should only be found in church on Sunday mornings. However, the shape and function of the liturgy are not founded upon a specific culture or people. Rather, it is transcultural, which means it easily fits the needs of every context and faith tradition. While pastors understand that each visit is unique, the biblical character of the liturgy taken into a pastoral conversation never needs to fit into a specific cultural paradigm.

The church has many different orders and rites to help visitors share God's word, sing, pray, praise, and give thanks during a visitation. But the use of written forms is not the only way that visitations are liturgical. Listening to a parishioner's needs, a conversation about family, a devotion based on a Scripture reading, a prayer from the heart, or giving a blessing—in these ways visits become liturgical. Each act cares for the soul in a particular way. Whether the plan for visitation is formal or fluid, there is always some form of liturgical character in the sense that there is order. Order is imperative so pastors know how to rightly apply God's word. Order is imperative so that the gospel shared makes sense for the one who receives it.

Visitation need not consist of using the historic forms and liturgies of the church exclusively. Natural conversation is vitally important in order to explore the real content of life—the true condition of the soul and its needs. Conversation is the great means of sharing, the means by which our stories take shape. Conversation liberates the soul and is the driving force for understanding how God's word can be prescribed as the remedy. This best occurs in one-on-one pastoral situations where the individual has the opportunity to elaborate on specific needs and burdens.

While these conversations may be about most anything or everything, they, too, take place within the church. Therefore, it is important that visitors keep the goal of God-pleasing soul care for the sake of the church in view. God is active in these conversations, whether they take place in a park, on the street, or in a restaurant. Spiritually speaking, these conversations are "within the church," no matter where the conversation happens to take place. The main objective of purposeful visitation always includes a disposition toward the betterment of the individual soul and, ultimately, the greater community of the church.

Though visitation is not liturgical in essence, it is in function. Separating the pastoral visit from the liturgical function would mean taking away what is essential to the liturgy—namely, the life-giving word of God. For example, the apostle Paul's desire to see how the churches were faring was not out of personal curiosity. No, rather, he asked so that he might continue to minister and support the needs of the faithful. So it is with our visitation today. God is piercing into the here and now ready to pour out the words of eternal life.

At times, this happens when the pastor knows specific needs that require intentional care. Other times, a conversation that begins rather informally will lead to the discovery of immediate spiritual needs. In either situation, the Lord comes to his people through those he has put in *that* place at *that* time. From the altar to the mouths and hearts of humans, the gifts of Christ become the gifts given to our neighbor through us. They are gifts of mercy, life, compassion, and forgiveness. It's the liturgy of life—nothing more and nothing else than a recapitulation of his life in our lives. We bear his presence in our bodies.[9]

God's Comfort through Listening

Visiting Carol after each life-changing tragedy became more and more difficult. Her grief intensified as her life became more broken and chaotic. I felt increasingly helpless each time I rang her doorbell. Yet, there I was, poised to take my seat in her living room and join her in her grief. That's what pastors do. Even more, that's what Christians do because that's what Christ does.

She sat on the living room couch and I in a chair by the fireplace. As always, I had my *Pastoral Care Companion* book which includes biblical texts, occasional prayers, and familiar liturgical recitations. These tools were at my disposal when I visited, but, honestly, I used them only sparingly. Most of the time, I simply listened. I listened to her share her heart-felt grief and unbearable pain. I listened to her groans toward God as she told me how defenseless and vulnerable she felt without her husband and sons. She couldn't understand why God would take away the three most important men in her life.

Week after week, I sat and listened to Carol. She began to tell me stories about her childhood, her life as a daughter, a wife, and a mother. She told me about her good and bad memories. But mostly, she talked about how it was her Lord that sustained her through all of it. She realized that God's great suffering is not just a story told, but a story lived. As we talked and reflected on God's story that she knew so well, she began to frame her life stories into God's redemption story. His story was her healing balm. His story of grace brought order into her chaotic, broken narrative of loss and grief.

Regular visits with Carol were important, especially since her loneliness came suddenly and overwhelmingly. She enjoyed the company, but she also wanted someone with whom to share her grief. It was more important to her that she had the opportunity to share her struggles rather than glean out of her pastor some sort of quick fix for her situation. She needed to grieve, and she could do that best through her story of grief. Much of her comfort came through the retelling of her life story and the discovery of God's intervention during other times she experienced grief and sorrow.

The Art of Listening

When I was a young pastor just beginning my journey in the ministry, I understood the value of visitation, but I wasn't sure what a good or productive visit looked like. I often got too caught up in thinking about what I should say and how choosing the right words to speak might make or break the visit in terms of effectiveness. I worried that if I didn't mention the right things, then I wasted my time and the time of the person I came to visit. It's safe to say that most of what I thought made a good visit depended on the visitor's strengths and skills, how he handled himself, and what spiritual direction he chose to share.

Through the school of experience, I realized that I would never be able to quantify the effectiveness of visitation. Nor was the visitation's success reliant on what I was able to say or accomplish.

Instead, visitation—whether to homebound members, to visitors to the church from the community, to delinquent persons, or to families or individuals for any number of reasons—must have listening as the primary goal. Listening invites the sharing of stories, which becomes fundamental to understanding hopes, feelings, needs, and whatever else might be beneficial to individual pastoral care. Listening is the doorway to understanding the truth about those whom pastors serve and the best way to grasp the condition of the soul.

Listening builds relationships by showing care and concern over experiences. Listening makes others feel more appreciated and wanted, as it helps build a foundation for trust. Listening makes the storyteller feel more human. It makes people feel that their issues have meaning and are important enough to be heard by others. Engaged listening shows the one being visited that what they say matters and is taken seriously. Listening is hard but vital work for the pastor. First and foremost, the pastor should address each visitation as an opportunity to listen.

Pastors sometimes fall into the bad habit of talking too much or, more precisely, talking when they should just listen. This is understandable since pastors are taught that ministry is about sharing the gospel, and in order to accomplish this task, the pastor must say something. And besides, pastors are fixers. They are taught to address problems and find a good and proper remedy as quickly as possible. Pastors quickly forget they are called to listen first, listen for as long as it takes, and then speak in rhythm with God's healing word.

There is an art to listening and, like any art, it takes practice to improve. Perhaps the most important part of becoming a better listener is remembering that what people have to say is important. It doesn't matter who the person is; that person's story is important and is worth the time to listen. Listening provides a doorway into the person's situation and helps us stand in their shoes—to see things from their point of view.

Stories take shape and the listener, in a way, becomes a part of it. He has one ear listening to the person and the other ear listening to the word of God. Pastors listen for opportunities to inter-twine God's story of love and redemption in the individual's life narrative. Active listening combined with intentional individual visitation helps to reveal needs that aren't usually brought out in group contexts or through the exchange of pleas-antries at a social event.

Listening for More to the Story

Georgia is a kind and giving servant who is a member of the congregation I serve. She is a mis-sionary at a seminary library in Kenya, Africa on furlough back in the states. Georgia is a strong and faithful Christian who spends months at a time in Kenya. She knows church doctrine quite well and she cares deeply for those she serves. While stateside, Georgia visits congregations around the country, sharing her experiences in Africa and raising money for her mission endeavors. While in Kansas City, she spends time with friends at church, attends Bible study and worship faithfully, and always has a big smile on her face. She has a jovial personality that is infectious. One can't help but smile back at her and react favorably to her positive and optimistic attitude.

However, as her pastor, I know a different side of Georgia that many do not. And this knowledge came by way of getting to know her better in a one-on-one setting. I've gotten to know the exceptional needs of her soul through active and intentional listening. There is no secret to it. I just listen and allow her to return to her story. Each time, I receive a little more insight as she adds a piece here or there. The bigger picture comes together and themes emerge. Then, I focus on these specific themes as they affect each of the life-stories she shares. A diagnosis of the soul's condition emerges and a proper application of God's word comes into focus as the remedy. Only after knowing the story and understanding the soul's condition can

I properly apply God's word. Listening is foundational to individual pastoral care and remains key to effective pastoral visitation.

Georgia is often sad and consumed with grief over matters that involve her family. They aren't as closely knit as they use to be. And things have continued to unravel to a greater extent after her arrival to Kansas City from Texas after her husband passed away suddenly. She moved to Kansas City to be closer to family, but that didn't work out as she had hoped. Family relationships became strained and despair quickly set in. Her stories reveal a loneliness that one would not expect from a person who portrays such a joyful demeanor around others.

She begins by sharing how her sadness is a result of how others have treated her. Then, as the conversation continued, she admits that she hasn't handled situations as she should. More than once, during follow-up visits with Georgia, she acknowledged that she spoke harsh words or didn't act in a Christian way. Listening to Georgia share her grievances helped her realize that she needed God's mercy and forgiveness. Together, our conversations revealed parts of her story that brought to light the whole truth. Georgia's sadness was not just about a strained family relationship imposed by others. It was about the guilt and sadness she felt for what she did to contribute to it. Here is where the liturgy of the Divine Service becomes essential to this particular visit.

Georgia desired to confess her sins and received God's absolution. My faith tradition has a rite of individual confession and absolution that the pastor and the penitent speak together. The way these words appear in the confession rite is not essential to the forgiveness of sins. Instead, they serve to direct the penitent to the sins that weigh heavy on the heart and then to receive God's forgiveness through the words of the pastor.

"In the stead and by the command of my Lord Jesus Christ, I forgive you all your sins in the name of the Father and of the Son and of the Holy Spirit."

These words are not the pastor's words. This is not the pastor's forgiveness. These words belong to God. It is God's forgiveness because it is God's word. "As the Father has sent me, even so I am sending you. ... Receive the Holy Spirit. If you forgive the sins of any, they are forgiven them; if you withhold forgiveness from any, it is withheld" (John 20:21–23). The liturgy of individual confession and absolution opened up a way for Georgia to speak her sins and receive the sweet salve of Christ's mercy.

Georgia's story is incomplete if we only know the missionary part—the joys and the challenges of serving the Lord in a foreign country. Her greater story reveals needs from deep within her soul that take time to discover and properly understand. I would have never known that Georgia also suffered from culture shock. No, not culture shock from entering the mission field in Africa, but rather culture shock from returning to her home country. She feels more comfortable in Africa than she does in the United States. I would never have guessed.

This challenge also remained at the forefront of our visits together as yet another liturgical refrain entered our conversation. This time the liturgy took the shape of Psalm 46: "Be still, and know that I am God. I will be exalted among the nations, I will be exalted in the earth! The LORD of hosts is with us; the God of Jacob is our fortress" (Ps 46:10–11). The ancient liturgical rite used here is nothing more than a psalm for strength prayed amid weakness. God's word speaks, and we listen.

Listening Again

Visitation invites companionship and therefore is ready-made for the sharing of stories. Eugene Peterson says that the pastor is God's spy, searching out ways of grace. The pastor and the one being visited combine stories and create a macro-narrative of sorts that involves God's intervention into the life of humankind. The pastor listens, helps arrange the data, calls attention to unnoticed material, and suggests the rearrangement of a sentence here, the change of a preposition there.[10] In this way, pastoral visitation is a minimal act. The pastor is not doing much. God is on the scene before, during, and after the conversation. The Holy Spirit is the primary activist within the conversation. The pastor is merely calling attention to what is already there through the skill of listening.

By virtue of his vocation, the pastor makes sure the material of God's divine story is brought into the visitation conversation. Personal stories are unique but never separated from God's active intervention—whether the story is favorable or tragic. With that, pastors invite people to tell their personal stories and offer themselves as skilled collaborators. Those who pastors visit will not always be willing participants and, truthfully, there is not much the pastor can do about that.

But what a pastor can do is follow up and invite dialogue again. Perhaps the sharing of one's narrative never takes shape. Maybe it eventually bears fruit. Either way, the pastor should not evaluate the visit's effectiveness based on how much one discovers through dialogue. God is at work accomplishing his will no matter what the pastor thinks about its productivity. Visitors can take comfort in knowing that God is responsible for the result. Again, pastors are called to visit the people. The results are left to God.

I have spent many hours listening to Carol and Georgia share their stories. I have asked a question or two here and there. But mostly, I let them talk. I let them take the conversation wherever they want it to go. A conversation that builds meaningful relationships and helps visitors understand the metanarratives of those they serve is so much more than superficial banter. Do not underestimate the value of telling stories. This is part of applying meaningful soul care to individuals whose lives inevitably intersect with the Lord's divine narrative. Remember, the pastor is always listening to the condition of the soul. At the same time, the pastor is always listening to God's word so that it can be applied rightly and effectively.

The liturgy of life with its ebb and flow of joyfulness and despair becomes intertwined with the liturgies we find in the church that tell the story of God's abundant grace. On more than one occasion, Carol revealed to me the meaningful place the church's liturgy had in her life. She found comfort in the repetition, the comforting litanies, and the familiar prayers. Recently, I asked her what her favorite part of the liturgy was. She said, without hesitation, the confession and absolution. "Pastor, the Bible reminds me that I'm a sinner in need of God's forgiveness. I confess my sins and God wipes them away. Even though I've spoken these words so many times, they still seem as fresh and new to me as when I spoke them in my childhood church in rural Missouri. God's word of forgiveness comforts me when I'm sad. They show me I have God's promise that I will see my sons and husband again."

All of us have a story. The church has a story and Jesus is at the center. Visitors have the blessed opportunity to hear and to tell both of them. The liturgy of God's word guides us in the endeavor of bringing them together, making God's story of redemption our very own.

Part II

Pastoral Resources

CHAPTER 4

Preparing for Pastoral Visitation: Things to Consider

THE BASICS FOR MAINTAINING A HEALTHY relationship between the pastor and the congregation are not complex. This healthy relationship is an essential foundation for effective pastoral care. Matthew Harrison in his book *Letters from a Pastor's Heart* mentions three important keys: preach a good sermon, visit the people, and be visible in the community.[11]

He's right; it's not complex. Healthy relationships depend on good communication. All three keys build on that one important fundamental. It's not enough, however, to know what makes for good and healthy relationships: we must also be able to put these keys into practice. How does one carry out the function of preaching a good sermon? How can one become more visible in the community? And, for the purpose of this book, how does one go about effectively visiting members in the church and the community? Putting these keys into practice forms the art of pastoral care.

All three of these keys are interrelated. They're most effective when they are put into practice with the other. Visitation produces the fodder for good preaching. Being visible in the community will help establish relationships that may lead to visitation. Good preaching relies on knowing the people and knowing the community. All three keys are dependent upon each other.

In *The Pastor: A Memoir*, Eugene Peterson illustrates this point by telling a story about his seminary days in New York City. Each seminarian had a fieldwork assignment for acquiring experience and education within the parish setting. He and several other seminarians were assigned to Madison Avenue Presbyterian Church, where the famed preacher, George Arthur Buttrick served as pastor.

One Sunday afternoon, Peterson and the others were invited to the pastor's home for conversation. One student asked Buttrick what was the most important thing he did to prepare for preaching a sermon. Perhaps the young theology students assumed the preacher might tell them his method of studying the biblical text or a new technique for effective delivery. Instead, they got a pragmatic lesson in the care of souls. His answer: "For two hours every Tuesday and Thursday afternoon, I walk through the neighborhood and make home visits. There is no way that I can preach the gospel to these people if I don't know how they are living, what they are thinking and talking about. Preaching is proclamation, God's word revealed in Jesus, but only when it gets embedded in conversation, in a listening ear and responding tongue, does it become gospel."[12]

Each pastoral care touchpoint strengthens the other. Visitation helps fill in the lines of life's coloring book with vibrant hues that bring important narratives to light. The preacher proclaims to individual souls who trudge down life's path in different ways. He must understand the condition of the soul and learn what makes up the various stories of those he serves, so that he may be equipped to minister to the individual parts of Christ's holy body—the church.

We visitors must also focus on how we can better prepare and carry out the ministry of visitation to others. A prepared and informed pastor is better equipped to carry out effective care of souls. In this chapter, I will share some practical ways for preparing to make pastoral visitation. I will also illustrate how visitations take place, especially with an eye toward modern challenges that face pastors today. Lastly, I will review ways pastors can train others for the task of visitation—especially lay visitation.

Preparation: Creating a Plan

Proper preparation is an important way to overcome the obstacles that often inhibit the pastor's ability to carry out visitation effectively. These obstacles fall into two categories: external and internal. External obstacles include the large amount of time it takes to make home visitations, the travel time between visits, and the demand of other duties that pull the pastor in many different directions. These obstacles will require visitors to plan out activities for each day during the week and make time management a priority especially so that the visitor's family and personal needs for self-care don't suffer.

The second obstacle, the internal obstacle, tends to be more at the heart of the visitor's primary challenge. Because visitors are human, we get nervous or become timid. The prospect of confrontation is always a possibility, and most people try to avoid those situations as much as possible. We aren't exactly sure what awaits on the other side of that door we are about to approach. Will they have tough questions we aren't sure how to answer? Are they preparing to do battle and argue over festering disagreements? Will the visit make the person feel nervous or, worse yet, disrupted and agitated? Visitation involves a certain level of risk. We aren't exactly sure what to expect, and that can give the visitor pause. The courage to carry out visitation can be challenging to muster when the unknown awaits. Every pastor has most certainly experienced this type of reluctance.

I still remember my first visitation as a new assistant pastor right out of the seminary. The senior pastor gave me a list of shut-ins, a list of sick and hospitalized, a list of church leadership, a list of prospective members, and a list of delinquent members. He told me to make a plan to visit all those on the lists. He didn't explain to me how to go about making these visits or which list to take up first. No, instead, he simply gave me names and left it up to me.

For some reason, and I'm still not sure why, I started to plan visits to the delinquent members first. Perhaps I thought they were the most in need, the furthest away from heaven, and that I could swoop in, make a good impression, and even set them back on the right path. Perhaps the new, young, and energetic pastor can save them from certain doom.

I didn't anticipate how nervous I would be until I got in the car and started to make my way to the first delinquent member's house. I had made visits before as a student—I had made visits with my mom many times, inviting neighbors to our church Vacation Bible School. But this was different. I was now a pastor. I realized I didn't have any real information about who I was visiting and why they stayed away from church. I hardly knew anything about the church I was serving. Nerves nearly overcame me, and I almost abandoned the visit.

To help combat both external and internal obstacles that tend to get in the way of effective pastoral visitation, it is helpful to create and implement an action plan. A plan will help the pastor stay organized, keep accurate records, manage time, and focus on essential needs and concerns. It doesn't matter what the plan is so much as there is a plan to begin with. Here are a few suggestions.

Create a Visitation List

Make a list of every member of the parish that includes their address, phone number, email, information about their family, any church ministries they are involved in, and upcoming milestones. Prioritize this list by creating categories that include regular attenders, irregular or delinquent attendees, shut-ins, and prospects. Many churches use organizational software that keeps track of basic membership information including notes for categories. I, however, find it helpful to keep my own records. I create individual folders for each family. I add dates visitations take place and follow-up phone or email contacts. I take notes about spiritual needs, family situations/concerns within the household, illnesses, and hospitalizations. With a few short lines, I summarize important narratives that bring everything from joy to despair. Essentially, I log everything I want to remember including favorite hymns and Bible verses. Note: this is highly sensitive material that includes pastoral observations, diagnoses, and plans for spiritual treatment. These folders must be safely secured to maintain the highest degree of confidential integrity. No one, including church leaders or employees, should ever have access to them. They should be destroyed if the pastor leaves to serve another ministry.

Make Initial Contact

Try to make phone contact with each church member. I suggest calling rather than email or text. Conversations are more intimate and help individuals to hear the pastor's inviting tone. Here, the conversation may extend to talking about family, job, background, church involvement (without asking them to get involved—at least not during this conversation), and any upcoming life events. The objective here is to get to know the membership and set the stage for important conversations that may need to occur in the future. Don't forget to jot down details that will be important to remember in your member folder. If you cannot talk to each person in the household, try to talk to at least one of them. This way, you can get a general idea of personal narratives and needs, which hopefully take shape through familiarity as time goes on.

Ask to Visit

Make your inquiry more than an offer, but an actual ask. For example, "I would like to sit down with you and your family and visit. May I please set up a time with you to come and visit with you in your home?" If you kindly offer a visit, they may be inclined to say that they are not in need of a visit. "It's okay, pastor, we are doing just fine. There's no reason to take up your valuable time." Ask them if they will allow you to come and visit. Mention that you are excited about the prospect of seeing them and demonstrate how this is important to you. The fact is that visitation is important. The individual care of each member of the body of Christ is our priority because each person is loved by Jesus, who leaves the ninety-nine in the hill country to search for the one lost sheep (Matt 18:12). Visitors do more than offer individual care; they carry out this good and proper work. Some will not allow the visitor to come to the house. They may be more comfortable with coming to visit at the church. Meeting at church is a fine way to get to know individuals within the church family. But, whenever possible, demonstrate a Christ-like willingness to come into their midst—into their sacred space—like Jesus demonstrates so many times in the New Testament. This action speaks to the visitor's eagerness to meet people where they are by bringing care and comfort to their doorstep.

Prepare to Make the Visit

Having a plan going into the visitation will help alleviate stress brought on by many of the internal and external obstacles mentioned above. Here are a few suggestions to help minimize some personal deterrents visitors must face.

First, map out your day. Ensure that if you are planning multiple visitations during the day or evening you schedule them by geographical location. This will help the visitor maximize personal time and resources.

Second, schedule enough time for each visitation. The care of souls cannot be rushed. Even more important, the one receiving care should not feel as if they were not afforded enough time and attention. On the other hand, pastors can out-stay their welcome. For home visitations, I suggest the visit to be no more than hour in length, unless the person asks for more time.

Third, create a purpose for the visit. It might help to put together a visitation series or theme which may include a devotional prayer service,[13] and, perhaps, a small memorable token like a cross, tract, or booklet that is left with the family. These items serve as a reminder of the visit and help members call to mind the visit's purpose. As mentioned previously, getting to know members, their stories, and their struggles is vitally important. However, having a purpose that involves a routine may add value to the visitation—especially if the visit is for a particular purpose. Creating a devotion or Bible study is not essential. However, some might expect the pastor to include a purpose with the visit. Also, having a purpose gives the pastor a specific reason for visiting.

Fourth, pray. Before entering the home, say a prayer. Ask God for strength and clarity. Ask for patience, that God would send his Holy Spirit and give you the wisdom to say nothing when listening is required and to speak the truth in love when the time is right. Pray for them. Pray that your time together is fruitful and productive for the sake of the body of Christ. Pray that they are given a receptive heart to receive God's instruction and encouragement. Pray for God's peace and joy—that they accompany the conversation and remain with the household.

Making the Visit

St. Paul tells the church in Rome how he intends to come to them: "I know that when I come to you I will come in the fullness of the blessing of Christ" (Rom 15:29). Visitation is more than a social encounter; it is the method by which God brings something special—his blessing. All visitations are unique, except for one thing: God himself is delivered right into the home through God's instruments who carry along his word and blessing. This truth should give us strength and courage to breach the doorposts of our neighbor. Visitors have a life-giving word to share. "For the word of the LORD is upright, and all his work is done in faithfulness" (Ps 33:4). But how do we go about sharing this word?

It's impossible to set down a single guideline for visitation. Each occasion will bring its own set of challenges and produce its own set of rules. There is never a "one-size-fits-all" answer to how pastors are to visit congregational members. Here, I will suggest a few practical elements to establish a general framework for visitors. This framework can be adapted to fit any context. (In the next chapter, I will explore specific visitation scenarios with homebound members, prospective members, delinquent members, and the like.) Here are four points to keep in mind while making visitations.

Pray in the Driveway

The first thing I do when I pull into the driveway or parking lot is pray. Yes, I already mentioned that, but it's worth repeating. Before every visitation, no matter the situation or purpose, I begin with a simple personal prayer while still sitting in my car. There is nothing particularly specific about this prayer other than including the elements I suggested above.

Along with the general preparations made for the visit, there might be a notable discussion point or two that I like to rehearse in my head. I try to approach the visitation without preconceived notions or a rigid agenda. A hard and fast agenda may be necessary in some cases. However,

I find that detailed agendas bind conversations too much and may inhibit topics the individual wants to address. Remember, visitation is for the soul care of the other. Allow them to set the course. You are there to listen and act as a guide when necessary. The individual may have a previously unknown spiritual concern they want to address. It is important for the visitor to be prepared and expect the unexpected.

Make Your Intentions Clear

During the general introductory portion of the conversation, I make the purpose for which I am visiting clear. [14] For example, I'm visiting because they are new in the area, and I was happy to see them in church on Sunday. Or, I might say I'm visiting because I haven't seen them at worship for a while and I'm concerned. Or, I'm visiting because this is a part of my annual routine of pastoral care. There are countless ways to communicate the general purpose of the visitation that will hopefully alleviate feelings of fear or concern about what might be the pastor's purpose for making a personal appearance at the home. The initial purpose is communicated while setting up the visit.

However, it helps to remind them to help alleviate any kind of confusion or suspicion.

Listening

After exchanging a few pleasantries and sharing the purpose for the visit, it's time to focus on the most important part of visitation—listening. I say the most important because listening is the foundation on which all pastoral care is built. Pastors must be good listeners first; otherwise, we might jump to wrong conclusions and unintentionally steer the conversation away from the primary problem. Listen to what they say and what they don't say. Listen for what to pray for at the end of the visit. Listen to the intimate details of family struggles or strife at work. The kitchen table or the living room couch are sacred spaces where the pastor listens with one ear to the needs of the individual and with the other to the voice of Jesus in the Scriptures.[15] Here is the advantage of the pastor being in the home of the individual. This is their place of security, and it has been my experience that it is also the place where parishioners are most comfortable sharing what is truly troubling their soul. Listening becomes the essential starting point. It gives the pastor the opportunity to come alongside this child of God and clearly articulate how Jesus comes to heal the broken-hearted and bind up festering wounds. With our ears, we hear stories that draw pictures of what those we care for need. The simple act of listening establishes the basis for attentive diagnosis of the spiritual condition and intentional treatment. Treatment comes through the healing word that God the Father provides in the blessed gift of Jesus through the power of the Holy Spirit. Listening, diagnosis, and application involves the art of discernment and is a skill that takes time to learn. The only way to sharpen these pastoral skills is to practice them. Books and theories cannot adequately prepare the pastor like good old-fashioned experience.

Conclude with Prayer and Blessing

Near the conclusion of the visit comes the fourth point I desire to accomplish: prayer and blessing. First, let's address the issue of prayer. Because I like to pray specific petitions that include the spiritual matters discussed during the visit, my prayers often include a petition *ex corde* (from the heart). This is not to say prayers written out ahead of time have no value.

On the contrary, oftentimes I include an appropriate prayer that I find in the *Pastoral Care Companion*, which lists prayers categorically. These prayers guide my thoughts and help me find words that I might change or alter to fit the individual's current situation. I prefer these prayers because they are built around God's very words. They are clear and specific especially when our impromptu attempts to find the right words falter.

The Psalms are particularly useful as prayers. Psalms have different categories like praise, wisdom, and thanksgiving. These categories help us fit them into a specific context. For example, psalms of lament give words to sufferers who may not know what to say during times of great distress. So, the chief function of the psalms of lament is that they put prayers into the mouths of sufferers and help them define the agony upon their hearts. "The Spirit himself intercedes for us with groanings too deep for words" (Rom 8:26b). They provide a framework for times of crises and grief that guide the sufferer from the misery caused by darkness and despair to the light of Christ and the joy of the Savior's substitutionary atonement.

And while this movement touches individuals psychologically and the community of the faithful liturgically, the transition from hurt to joy, crisis to faith, grief to relief, is a profoundly spiritual one. It is God's activity to bring sinners into the midst of his grace. Other portions of Scripture also accompany prayer as either a part of the prayer itself, or as a reading before the prayer begins. The Scripture or psalms that accompany the prayer can be chosen based on the visitor's assessment of spiritual needs. The right word spoken at the right time lies at the heart of faithful soul care. Pastors need to know the right word to speak. Therefore, pastors need to prayerfully meditate and take to heart careful study of God's word. Using a daily lectionary with psalms for use in the morning and the evening help imprint the word on the mind and the heart.

Using God's word as prayer and comfort is the basis for the mindful liturgical flow of visitation that brings the hearer into the presence of God's word. After conversation, after reflection on challenges and hardships, it's God's turn to speak to us. God speaks and we listen. We speak to him our hopes, needs, and desires through prayer. Now, in his word, God talks back to us, which is indicative of his loving nature. Our prayers are a conversation from God to us, back to God. His blessing is an enactment from God's promise through the giving of the blessing to the receiver. This gospel enactment of blessing is a divinely-given spiritual power granted as a performative declaration from Christ.

After the prayers conclude, I give a blessing before I depart. I never really thought to incorporate blessing during visitation until I attended a pastors' conference led by Dr. John Kleinig in Nebraska the fall of 2009. Before this time, it hadn't occurred to me how valuable and powerful a few simple words, a consecration from the Lord that opens heaven's gifts through gospel enactment, can be. Kleinig emphasizes that we can take God with us wherever we go and show his hidden glory to the world around us.[16] Blessing reveals what is hidden to the troubled soul—God places his name on what belongs to him. Receivers of blessing are enabled to hear for themselves that the Lord protects, equips, and empowers in a world that is often blind to God's goodness.

Sometimes this blessing is a part of the prayer and other times it is separate. Most of the time, but not always, the blessing I use is the Aaronic Benediction, inserting the name of the person I am visiting into the blessing. I love the imagery this ancient and liturgical blessing gives of the Lord turning his face toward the recipient and granting peace that flows directly from heaven. If possible, I place my hands directly upon their head and I say this, "The LORD bless you and keep you; The LORD make his face shine upon you and be gracious to you; the LORD lift up his countenance upon you and give you peace" (Num 6:24–26). The opportunity to touch, where or when appropriate, personalizes God's word of blessing and helps to demonstrate how this benediction is specifically for them.

God positions himself toward those who receive a blessing which makes visitation an appropriate time to do so. Eugene Peterson illustrates the posture of blessing by referencing a book called, *The God Who Stands, Stoops and Stays.* God stands—he is foundational and dependable; God stoops—he kneels to our level and meets us where we are; God stays—he sticks with us through hard times and good, sharing his life with us in grace and peace.[17] And because our Lord comes to us in blessing, it is entirely appropriate to use blessing at the conclusion of visitation—since most recognize blessing to come at the end of the worship service.

Visitation is also an appropriate time to teach souls the way to pray and bless. The language of prayer does not come naturally. The disciples asked Jesus to teach them how to pray like John taught his disciples (Luke 11:1). We learn to speak a different language in prayer. We speak in ways that are foreign to our day-to-day conversations. We learn to formulate petitions that include things like thanksgiving, confession, and supplication. Therefore, praying during the visitation also acts didactically so that others may mimic prayers.

The same for teaching blessing. Unfortunately, blessing is not something many people think they can or should do. Since blessing is a performative utterance, a speech act that demonstrates and encapsulates the gospel located upon another person, blessing is not an act that only belongs to pastors. Individuals have the privilege to be close (in proximity) to their family. They tuck their children into bed at night, they encourage them in their times of need, and, even with their spouse, they are given the opportunity to converse about the joys and the struggles of the day.

These, then, become appropriate times for prayer and blessing with family. And since the family is so close in proximity, a simple word of

God's blessing is easily placed upon them. For example, at bedtime, a child might be put to bed with these words, "The Lord bless you and keep you throughout this night as you sleep. God grant you a peaceful rest while He sends His Holy Angels to protect you—in the name of the Father, and of the Son, and of the Holy Spirit." Even more, children can be taught to bless parents in return. They could even use the same blessing given to them. In family life together, there is more time and opportunity to carry out these treasured benedictions and explain their meaning.

However difficult and time-consuming we may find visitation to be, we as pastors understand that the ministry is active. It moves from chancel to the home and back again. Our conversations with others form and inspire our prayers. Listening is the most important task during visitation. As we listen to the needs of others, the pastor soon discovers what to preach on Sunday morning and what to pray for in times of personal and corporate prayer. Listening is the giving of ourselves during conversation. So is prayer.

In intercession, we use our active faith for the sake of others. We also show our love for those we pray for as we give ourselves spiritually to them. It isn't much to make small talk about the weather and such things. But what if our conversations included petitions of need brought before the heavenly throne? What if we wrap the parishioner's greatest concerns in prayer with a word from our Lord in a psalm? What if we include a petition that called them by name and spoke directly to their situation?[18] Now, see how personal everything becomes. See how the Lord intersects with the discussion, wrapped into the very words, and the opportunity now arises to accentuate simple petitions with a direct blessing from the Lord. From our petitions to God, spoken by his children as answering speech, to the blessing of Christ, actively dispensed to the receiver, prayer and blessing come together.

Prayer and blessing are not intrinsically the same. However, the dimension of prayer between God and humankind acutely lends itself to something else that can come next. That second thing is a blessing which is a gospel enactment from the Lord through the giver to the receiver. The blessing brings everything back to where it all begins—God's grace and mercy for the sake of those he loves.

In summary, visitation brings the pastor to the door of the parishioner. Then, conversation draws forth joys, concerns, and even sorrows as the pastor actively listens and empathizes. The liturgical flow within the home's sacred space continues when prayers are offered up, imploring the Lord to intercede. Then, the full delivery of Christ is brought back to the parishioner through a word of blessing in which Jesus comes to touch lives and strengthen souls.

CHAPTER 5

Doing Pastoral Visitation: Making it Work

A NEW FAMILY OF FOUR MOVED INTO OUR AREA and joined our church. The day we received them into membership I told them I wanted to set up a time to come and visit. They were agreeable but also concerned that work commitments and the kids' club sports activities would prevent this from actually happening.

I called the husband first. No answer. I left a message. I called the wife and, again, no answer. I then texted the husband and he texted back the next day. I gave him some times I was available for visitation and he said he would have to check with his wife. After a few more text messages back and forth we finally settled on a day about three weeks away. When that day finally came, I texted once again to remind them of the visit. Unfortunately, one of the children's baseball games got rescheduled and they forgot to let me know. We rescheduled again for the next week.

The next week got cancelled too. The reason was the same as before. We tried the next week but a family emergency prohibited it. Finally, the next week, we were able to find a day to get together. It was hard to come by, but the visitation we planned weeks before finally happened.

Visitation affords many different opportunities to learn, teach, pray, and bless. Yet, in this day and age, getting the opportunity to visit homes is a challenge. In my twenty-one years in parish ministry, I have had to adapt to the ever-changing world and family dynamic. More of those I serve will not allow pastors to come and see them because they see this as generally unnecessary. Jobs and extracurricular activities have families scrambling from one event to the next. A large number of people screen phone calls or refuse to answer the doorbell. Telemarketers and package delivery systems have conditioned people to ignore their phone or the knock at their door.

On top of all this, many pastors struggle to make personal contact because face-to-face communication is becoming less and less the norm. Today, many people communicate mostly by email or text, thereby avoiding direct conversation. All of these factors and many others make pastoral visitation a major challenge in this day and age.

OTHER METHODS OF CONTACT

Home visitation is crucial but it is not the only means by which pastors can connect with parishioners. Other means of communication may help grease the wheel for a face-to-face visitation later. Here are a few other methods of contact pastors may utilize to lead to a more personal means of pastoral care in the future.

Voicemails

Calling members on the phone to set up a visit is the second step of the visitation plan discussed above. Visitors should be prepared to communicate through voicemail. I have discovered that most visitors, whether they are lay visitors or pastors, will encounter voicemail most of the time. When this happens, it's important to be friendly, inviting, and prepared. Here are a few suggestions.

First, make sure to leave a message every time. Don't hang up on the voicemail and expect that you will speak with them later. Chances are, they will continue to allow your call to go to voicemail since they are unclear about your reason for calling. People want to know what the phone call is about before deciding whether or not to call back.

Second, create a script. Let those you are trying to reach know why you are reaching out to them. For example, tell them, "I'm calling you today because I'm setting up home visitations to the entire church family, and I would like to make a time I can come and visit." State your reason and purpose for wanting to visit very clearly. Tell them that you look forward to speaking with them and that you are willing to reach out and call them again. It's a good possibility that the next time you call them they will not answer. When this happens, leave another message so that they are not in the dark as to why you are attempting to reach them. A second voicemail will also indicate that this is important to you and that they are important enough to go and visit.

Third, have a plan for those who do not respond by voicemail. Some will not respond by phone. This may not be their preferred method of communication. If they do not respond to voicemails, it's time to explore a different initial contact method, such as a hand-written note, an email, or a text message.

Emails

Computers and other modern devices have made spiritual care both easier and more difficult. Easier in the sense that reaching out to others has never been more convenient and accessible. More difficult because people rely less on personal contact for communication and more on digital means of sharing information from a distance. Effective spiritual care is met with the challenge of adapting to these alternative means of communication. While communication through email has its limits for carrying out spiritual care, it can still be an effective tool for visitors. If phone calls continue to be ignored, then an appropriately worded email may help. Here are some suggestions.

First, make it personal. Don't use a blanket email that includes multiple recipients. Emails that are not personal are less likely to have an impact. Statistics show that the global email spam rate for individuals worldwide is one out of every two emails.[19] Advertisers, marketing surveys, and even scammers bombard inboxes with all sorts of messages that will never be taken seriously. To make sure that members will read the email that pastors and other visitors send, make it personal. Use, "Dear _____," to introduce the missive. Don't be afraid to ask about family or a particular circumstance that they might be dealing with at the time. Perhaps you can share a little about yourself or your own family. Be friendly and inviting. You don't need to share too much. This email is not about you; it's about them.

Second, get to the point. Like with voicemails, clearly state your purpose. Email is a good way to directly and accurately communicate your purpose. Take time with your email and make sure that it states what you desire to communicate accurately and succinctly. A long, rambling email is not necessary.

Third, ask for a response. If you ask for a response by email, you will most likely get a response by email. Give the recipient times and days you are available for visitation. Ask them to choose one or two in their email response. If none of those times work, tell the person to let you know what times work best. Do everything you can to accommodate their time and date. You may have to set aside an evening, Saturday, or Sunday afternoon.

Fourth, follow up. If they do not respond, follow up with another email. Tell them that you have not received a response and ask if they received your previous email. It's possible that your email got lost amid an avalanche of other emails that the individual receives each day. If they don't respond again, try writing them a personal letter.

Letters and Notes

Personal, hand-written notes are an effective and touching way to connect with members. Not only can they be used to set up a line of communication that will hopefully include an in-person visit, they are also an excellent way to follow up after a visit. Notes that recognize anniversaries, birthdays, or important religious occasions show that you care and keep them in mind during their special times. They also help build relationships and connections that will hopefully open the door for other spiritual care methods later on.

When I graduated seminary, I received a call to serve as the assistant pastor of a congregation in the Kansas City area (where I now serve as senior pastor). The senior pastor at that time, R. Robert

Krueger, was a strict, tough, yet caring man who was proud of what he called his "old school" ways of practicing pastoral care. He wrote many thoughtful and heart-warming letters on his electric typewriter or spoke them into a Dictaphone for his secretary to type out on the computer. Members of our church family called these messages "Rev-O-Grams." Although he retired almost twenty years ago, church members still talk about receiving these notes from their beloved pastor.

Letters and notes leave a paper trail of words that can be treasured by recipients for years to come. I still have a box full of letters from Pastor Krueger I look through occasionally. I enjoy rereading his nuggets of spiritual direction and collegial advice he shared within those pages. Sometimes he wrote a note of thanks when he was grateful for something I did or a word of encouragement when I was struggling. I treasure these handwritten notes filled with wisdom given by a seasoned pastor—even after all of these years. Pastor Krueger went to heaven years ago, but I still feel that I have his wise counsel with me. Not only do caring letters foster relationships, but they also leave behind important spiritual care within their words.

Social Media

Social media has proven to be both a blessing and a curse. Its benefits include the ability to dispense information quickly and connect members to the community. Also, individuals share life experiences that include memorable times with family and friends, and moments that cause suffering and discouragement. These become opportunities for visitors to express concern and lend support. However, there are times when individuals put messages on social media that are unbecoming to them and the church. They share information from news media outlets or make comments we disagree with. Pastors should use much caution when responding to social media posts. If a particular concern arises, it may be more beneficial to use a different medium for communication to that individual. Here are a few considerations for pastors regarding the use of social media with visitation.

First, respond to all social media posts with care and compassion. Remember, your response can be seen by anyone who is friends with that person. Each response leaves an impression with not only the person who made the original post but also with many others. Keep kindness and thoughtfulness in mind before posting a response. You represent not only yourself but also the church you serve.

Second, respond privately if the social media post is sensitive in nature. A pastor friend of mine once told me that a member of the congregation he served posted an unflattering comment about the church on her Facebook page. When the pastor was alerted to the comment, he immediately called to speak to the person about the post privately. He addressed the issue over the phone, which prompted her to take down the unflattering post. The pastor then scheduled a visit with the woman, where they resolved the matter between them. This tactic was much more effective than if he were to respond on social media. It's entirely possible that an argument would commence and cause the situation to worsen.

Third, respond privately if there is a concern expressed without much information. On occasion, I have seen members use the "check in" feature on Facebook. In one particular instance I noticed a pregnant member checked into the local hospital well before her due date. I messaged her privately and asked if there was anything wrong. She responded that she was in labor and that they needed to do an emergency C-section. I rushed to the hospital to be with her and her family before and during the procedure. Thankfully, everything turned out well for both mother and baby. Social media informed me that one of my members needed help.

Fourth, if you see a social media post that brings you concern for the person's physical, mental, or spiritual welfare, reach out to that person privately and immediately. Most people will likely make caring comments but do nothing else. If there is cause for concern, contact that person directly, listen to them, and then decide what to do for their well-being.

Voicemails, emails, letters, and social media are useful means for communicating and receiving information, making initial contact with members, following up after a personal visit, and fostering already established relationships. Although in-person visitation is more ideal, these methods are still useful to visitors who desire to connect with others. What is more, they can also be used to communicate spiritual concern, reminders that individuals are kept in prayer, the writing or speaking of prayers, and the sharing of a blessing. For example, if one is leaving a voice message, that message can be more than just informational. That message can express concern for them if they are experiencing despair, it can communicate that prayers are taking place on their behalf, and it can conclude with words of blessing and the honest portrayal of God's presence and gospel peace. Emails and letters can include a prayer individually tailored for their situation. In my experience, conversations that begin on social media or a friendly text message can blossom into opportunities to share prayers and blessings that allow for a visitation follow-up.

Visitation During a Pandemic

The onset of the Covid-19 pandemic in 2020 quickly changed nearly everything about life, including visitation. What was once as easy as walking through the hospital, nursing home, or assisted living facility main entrance became a process of taking temperatures and filling out forms. In some cases, visitations to facilities were strictly forbidden.

I was astonished to see how quickly pastors adapted and found new ways to share the gospel amid what amounted to a global shutdown. However, these new and creative ways presented their own set of challenges to the church. How can the church be the church and do what the church does without the gathering together of the ones who make up the church? How can the church worship without worshipers? How can pastors visit without actually being present with them?

At the height of the pandemic, the husband of an elderly member with Alzheimer's was denied visitation to his bride. Every morning before the pandemic, he came to the nursing home, fed her breakfast, and they watched TV or talked until noon. He fed her lunch and then he went home. For seven years, he was the only one who fed her breakfast and lunch.

When he was no longer able to visit and feed her, she stopped eating. Slowly she wasted away, becoming thin and malnourished. Still, much to our dismay, they would not allow him to visit and feed her. The family stood outside her nursing home window, singing hymns, reading Scripture, and praying.

During her very last days, her husband was finally able to visit. Thankfully, they allowed me to visit as well. We prayed together, sang more hymns, and read from God's word. Usually, we would have Holy Communion together but by this time, she was not capable. I left her and her husband with a blessing and in the hands of their loving God. It wasn't long after that the Lord took home this precious woman who was, like so many, a casualty of this terrible pandemic.

Visitors sometimes have to take what we get. A pandemic is undoubtedly no exception. Hospitals and other care facilities all but deny access to pastoral visitation. With the inability to visit my people, I have allowed the sting of shame to fill my heart. Sometimes I can't shake the feeling that I'm not doing the job God has called me to do. The opportunity to come near in proximity to those I serve was stripped away. As time goes on, many feelings come over me. I've been angry. I've been sad. At times, I even begin to feel complacent about it all. I fear this is the new normal. I fear things will never be the same again.

Dear pastors, do not feel guilty for what we are unable to control. Keeping our distance during these challenging times may be necessary for our own health and well-being and those we serve. Don't forget, the church and your ministry still belong to God. "This God is our God for ever and ever: he will be our guide even unto death" (Ps 48:14 KJV). He is in control, and he remains Lord of the church—in good times and in bad. Though there are times we cannot be present like we desire, God still takes care of those he loves. Regardless of the circumstances, he is still at work through visitors even during pandemics. God still uses his valued instruments to bring the gospel of Jesus to the lives of his people. This means pastoral visitation still has purpose and meaning, although it may need to happen in different forms. Pastors still have the privilege of engaging in the vocation of visitation even during periods of physical separation.

How does the pastor carry out visitation during a pandemic? This method of the care of souls will require a few adjustments and some creativity, so it can take place from an appropriate distance.

Visit Outdoors

Plan for an outside visitation with members on the patio or deck of their home. Members who reside in community-type facilities usually have access to outdoor tables or benches. If they feel comfortable meeting in a wide-open space like a park, that could be arranged. However, it is important to have some privacy in the outdoor setting since sensitive issues may need to be addressed.

Visit at a Restaurant

In some areas, dine-in seating may not be possible. However, a restaurant may be a good place to at least connect with members and see how they are faring. If dine-in is available, seating is usually spread out and privacy is easier to come by. Lunch get-togethers can be an effective way to follow up with others concerning ongoing situations or to share ideas and advice.

Visit at Church

During a pandemic, many state and local governments may limit the number of people inside the church building. This makes it necessary for the pastor to visit individuals and families in smaller groups. Setting up appointments to meet at church may be the best way to carry out individual soul care in a safe manner during a pandemic. Online sign-ups may be used for small group Holy

Communion celebrations. Setting up appointments over the phone is also a useful tool.

Make Deliveries

A good way to contact members at their home is to deliver a devotional prayer book or hymnal. Entry into the house is not necessary. You may deliver information or an inspirational item in a bag, leave it on the door handle, and back away for a brief conversation at a distance. While this is not the best way to have a face-to-face conversation, this at least allows the pastor to express care and concern while at the same time connecting with church members in person. Perhaps have the congregation's youth make a small item that can be given as a religious keepsake. Perhaps have members of the congregation write notes that can be delivered at this time also. There are many good and beneficial possibilities for delivery bag items.

Make Virtual Visits

Technology has afforded the opportunity for pastors to use video platforms like Zoom or Facetime to connect with members when in-person contact may not be possible. Take advantage of the video features wherever available. Seeing someone's face is important. Facial expressions can tell the story of fear, concern, or illness. You, in turn, can show how much you care and understand the hardships they face. If at all possible, make the virtual visit the same as an in-person visit. Use Scripture, prayers, and a blessing—all the same as you otherwise would.

Make Phone Calls and Send Letters

There are a few advantages of using phone calls and writing letters during a pandemic. First of all, they are both easy and quick. Second, pastors can make more calls and write more letters than they can make visits in person. Phone calls and letters usually take less time to accomplish and the lack of travel is more efficient. Also, church elders or trained visitors within the church family can assist with making these points of contact as well as writing inspirational and encouraging notes to members. Don't forget: the writing of cards may be a good project for the church youth group to engage in.

It's quite an understatement to say that a pandemic brings difficult challenges to pastoral visitation. At a time when the church needs pastoral care the most, the most effective ways to carry out that care are stymied. This can bring despair to the hearts of members and pastors alike. The church is the embodiment of Christ. Christians are meant to be together in worship and community. The very identity of what the church is and who we are as the embodied church under the headship of Christ is indicative of a people who worship and serve with (in the presence of) one another. Christ is with us and we are with Christ. And when the body of Christ becomes disembodied, the very identity of the church is compromised. God's people are meant to be together.

Using alternative means to disseminate information, communicate care and concern for others, provide devotional and worship materials, and stay connected during times of separation will help churches and pastors navigate the murky waters of physical separation. The suggestions given above are not comprehensive and, admittedly, given the circumstances, less than ideal.

However, they do provide a good foundation to maintain a sense of connectedness during difficult times. This takes effort, but families need this.

The Training of Lay Visitors

Pastoral visitation's primary function is soul care to individuals in homes, hospital rooms, and the like. Yet, pastors are not pastors to a group of individuals but to a community that gathers around God's word and sacraments. The pastor is a pastor in and for the entire church community—the body of Christ. While we have defined pastors as visitors, they are not the only ones who can and should make visits within the congregation. A living and active community does not thrive when one person, the pastor, is taking care of the entire church singlehandedly, but rather when the community is actively supporting and caring for one another. Christians show the Savior's enduring love and act as Christ-like servants by demonstrating care for their neighbor. Visitation from one Christian to the other naturally flows from the active love Christians show to one another.

Pastors have the privilege to nurture the active demonstration of love by equipping the saints for this type of Christian service. God showers the entire church with gifts that, in turn, come with the expectation that every Christian use them responsibly for the sake of their neighbor. Putting these gifts to use will inevitably lead lay members into situations where they bring God's comfort and care through the mode of visitation. Here we need to ask two important questions:

> How does the pastor equip lay members to become responsible and effective visitors?

> In what ways is the visitation of a lay member different than the pastor's visitation?

The Basics of Training

Although this book's purpose is to focus on pastoral visitation, we would be remiss not to address the issue of lay visitation since the body of Christ lives, functions, and supports each other as a church family. Laypeople should be trained to visit members—especially those appointed or elected within the church to serve in spiritual leadership roles, such as elders or deacons. Since these roles are established in support of the pastoral office, lay visitation within these positions not only assists pastors in carrying out their duties, but also serves as another important means for spiritual care. I suggest two ways of training the members of the congregation, along with elders and deacons, for visitation: teach acts of service using visitation as a part of your regular Bible study and preaching, and intentionally train elders using tools geared explicitly toward lay visitation.

Teaching and Preaching Visitation

One of the primary functions of the pastoral office is to teach and preach the word of God. The taught and proclaimed word includes the law that shows sinners that they desperately need the gospel, which is the word of redemption for lost souls. Yet, included in teaching and proclamation, the word also serves a didactic purpose that directs Christians on how to live and serve. I'm not suggesting that every Bible study and every sermon have a visitation theme. No, rather, I hope to instill within you the importance of incorporating the Christian life, how to live it, and how to serve others through it into your Bible studies and sermons. Pastors can connect biblical theory to practical service through any study or sermon to show how Christians put God's comfort into motion for their neighbor. Ultimately, visitation is the incorporation of gracious acts of service from one member of the body of Christ to another. The Scriptures are teeming with examples of how the prophets and the apostles, and, of course, Jesus himself, brought love to the neighbor. Teaching and preaching are actively set into motion when pastors demonstrate and encourage the flock to listen to others' needs and share God's comfort as fellow believers who struggle together with the changes and chances of life. Visitation is taught by teaching and demonstrating the Christian life in light of the life of Christ.

Recently, our church family studied the Gospel of Luke on Sunday morning. The story of Zacchaeus the tax collector gave the class ample opportunity to reflect on the actions of Jesus who, unexpectedly, visited the home of a much-maligned man. As one might expect, discussion revolved around how Jesus loves everyone including those who society would least suspect deserves it. But the conversation did not end with Jesus's visitation; the class continued talking about how we, too, can demonstrate love like Jesus to those who might least expect it. One class member suggested that maybe the person we encounter is not one rejected by society but rather someone who would least expect us to visit them. This was perhaps what Zacchaeus might have thought about Jesus. "There is no way Jesus would ever come and see me. He doesn't know me, and he certainly doesn't care about me."

That member in Bible study gave the class, and subsequently, the entire congregation, an idea. Go and visit someone they might know but don't know too well, and get to know them better. The response was amazing. Each Sunday, as Bible class began, the participants told their stories of their friendly encounters with unsuspecting neighbors. They told how they just went over and knocked on the door and said, "I live down the street and I don't think we've ever met. I wanted to introduce myself." One by one, members told their stories. Some visits resulted in newly formed friendships and invitations to come to church. Some of those visits resulted in families joining our church and creating newfound bonds that will last a lifetime. This was no program that had people memorizing a script or key Bible passages. This was about two people meeting and getting to know each other's narratives. This was about people becoming a part of the other's story. This was about bringing others into the story of Jesus by connecting them to the community of the church through a simple act of kindness. The circle widens as God's love is demonstrated through the laity toward others.

Teaching and preaching about lay visitation may also include encouragement to incorporate the basic components of visitation: listening, prayer, and blessing. A basic structure—a liturgy of visitation, if you will—may help lay members focus on what is most important and not feel overwhelmed if they feel unqualified to diagnose spiritual distress and apply an appropriate treatment based on God's word. Lay members can still have an effective visitation ministry by being present, listening to narratives that include both struggle and joy, praying with and for that individual, and speaking a simple word of blessing, "The Lord bless you and keep you." They can be taught to listen for things they may want to ask if they can share with the pastor. Lay members can be taught the language of prayer so they don't feel unfit to pray *ex corde* (from the heart).

The idea is to create a culture of visitation within the church family so that the language of Christian service and God's people visiting one another are identified as one and the same. To teach this, pastors don't need to incorporate a dedicated program, a special Bible class, or a sermon series. Pastors need to routinely speak about the blessings of visitation—whether it be pastoral or lay visitation—as a vitally important way to express love toward the neighbor.

Training Elders and Deacons

There is a difference between pastoral visitation and the visitation of lay elders/deacons (or any other layperson, for that matter). Pastors are God's called servants, which, as we have already discussed, includes the identifiable vocation of visitor as found in the Scriptures. The pastor is trained to be attentive to the soul's condition and implement an intentional treatment founded upon God's word. The pastor has the primary duty of tending to the needs of the sheep and is held accountable to God for their care. Pastors are given the vocation of administration of the sacraments; these are a part of the curative means that God gives to forgive and strengthen his people. Added to this, no one knows the needs of the church family like the pastor. People will expect the pastor to be the one on the front lines of soul care during times of great distress. People expect their pastor to visit. For these reasons, pastoral visitation is vital for the congregation and must stand apart from lay visitation.

Yet, this is not to say that lay visitation has no rightful place within the church. Nor is it to say that spiritual leaders in the congregation should not be taught and trained to be visitors. On the contrary, lay leaders should be taught to visit in support of the pastoral ministry. However, it's not merely a friendly check-in to see how someone is fairing, though that is a valid reason to visit. No, instead, it's a meaningful encounter meant to build up the body of Christ with spiritual care and concern at its core.

The singular pastor, or the pastoral staff, can only make so many visits. For that reason, it is important to train a team of dedicated elders and deacons to extend the reach of spiritual care out into the parish family beyond what only one person (or just a few) can do. If properly trained, elders and deacons are an excellent means of care to the congregation and support for the church's overall ministry. Therefore, I suggest that elders and deacons be trained by pastors to visit members within their various needs.

There are effective training materials that can assist pastors in this endeavor. Some include video examples of visitation situations and case studies so that elders and deacons can practice within a group setting. Proper training materials will help pastors, elders, and deacons identify and practice the advanced skills needed to be effective. I include a few training titles in the annotated bibliography at the conclusion of this book. I encourage you to explore each resource and find the one that best fits your needs.

Keep in mind that elders and deacons are serving for the sake of the church outside of their usual vocation. If we ask them to do a job they are not trained to do, we set them up to fail at a ministry that is intended to help. They may become discouraged because they view their ministry as ineffective or too challenging to their skillset. Practicing in a group setting, starting off with calls that might be considered less hazardous, along with the pastor's encouragement will go a long way in helping elders and deacons become comfortable making visitations.

Conclusion

It requires patience and practice to improve any skill set. Pastoral visitation is no exception. The best way for pastors to become better visitors, and subsequently, better pastors is to go out and to minister where the flock lives. Get to know their struggles and their sufferings. Listen and understand what brings them joy and gives them strength to navigate the treacherous waters of this sin-laden world. Oswald Chambers warns that effective soul care cannot be learned from books. He tells a funny story about two men—an old sea captain and an author of a book on how to catch fish—going fishing. They stayed out for hours and the author didn't catch anything. The reason: he didn't have enough strength to put the line over the boat because he was too seasick to even try.[20] Books, like this one, can help us to prepare and understand the ins and outs from an academic point of view. However, nothing compares to the training of mind and body better than good old-fashioned doing.

CHAPTER 6

Pastoral Visitation: Five Situations

ONE EVENING WHILE I WAS DRIVING, A CAR came recklessly speeding toward me. It lost control, veered right in front of me, and violently ran into a large oak tree in the front yard of a house. I pulled over and approached the mangled wreckage.

The driver and front-seat passenger were unconscious. A paramedic also arrived on the scene and called 911.

We heard crying coming from the back of the vehicle. A young girl about ten years old, with her seatbelt still securely fastened, was crying out with pain. Her stomach was severely bruised from the accident. We helped her out of the back seat and laid her a safe distance from the wreckage.

I asked her if we could pray together. She said yes, and we prayed for her and the others in the accident. Not long after, the girl's mother arrived on the scene. The mother was the wife of the driver and the front-seat passenger was the girl's cousin. I told her I was a pastor. I listened to her loud groans of despair. I held her hand and stood by her side. I continued to pray out loud, and she concluded my petitions with an "amen" through her tears. The driver and the front-seat passenger died at the scene of the crash.

This was anything but an ordinary pastoral care situation. I had no idea God would put me in that place on that day to visit with strangers experiencing a terrible tragedy.

Visitation situations come in all sorts of shapes and sizes. Most visitations are planned events, while some are completely unexpected. Planned visits are *proactive* as pastoral care is brought to where the parishioner resides. Unplanned visits are *reactive* and often occur spontaneously wherever the pastor happens to be. Planned visits happen for a reason we already know. Unplanned visits happen out of the blue for any number of unknown reasons.

Whether visitation is planned or unplanned, reasons known or unknown, the aim of pastoral visitation remains the same: provide care for souls in extraordinary situations. It's impossible to plan for every scenario, like the one mentioned above. Yet, most pastoral visitation encounters usually fall into categories we might call common or routine. These are the visits pastors experience on a regular basis. However, while common, they are still as unique as the individuals pastors serve.

This chapter delves into five distinct visitation situations in which fundamental spiritual problems occur. Suffering and despair are addressed during visitation to the sick and dying. Fear and anxiety occur within a man who is visited before surgery. Loneliness and isolation are expressed as a reoccurring narrative of a shut-in. Unbelief and misbelief show themselves within a visit to a lost soul. And, shame and guilt manifest themselves when tragedy strikes a single mother. The spiritual problems are not limited to these situations but are couched within them to illustrate where pastors can expect to find them. You will notice that the maladies addressed will, at times, overlap since the fundamental principle of soul care often addresses the same problems manifested within different situations. The goal is to identify the spiritual needs and then consider ways pastors can effectively address these needs within the visitation context.

Situation 1: Visitation to the Sick and Dying (Suffering and Despair)

Pastors know that they will visit the sick and the dying. The sick and the dying know and expect that the pastor will visit. No other situation is perceived as more crucial and necessary than caring for those who are closest to heaven. For this reason, pastors are deployed into action as soldiers with boots on the ground to battle the forces of evil that create despair in the hearts of sufferers during these great times of need. Pastors have the greatest weapon at their disposal: the gospel. "For as we share abundantly in Christ's sufferings, so through Christ we share abundantly in comfort too" (2 Cor 1:5).

The sick and dying often wonder about the relationship between sin and sickness, especially when illness comes early in life. "Why am I suffering like this? What did I do to deserve this?" The devil is quick to deceive sufferers and trick them into thinking that somehow self-righteousness would have saved them or that God is vengeful and vindictive. These are lies. Christians live in a sin-filled world and have fallen, imperfect bodies that are susceptible to all sorts of disease or injury. Pastors do not visit to give answers to these questions. They visit to share the comfort that God promises through the mercy of Christ.

The problem of suffering besets those who despair over sickness and death. This is often the core spiritual malady pastors encounter at the bedside of the sick and dying.

"I don't want to die, pastor," whispered Evie as she lay almost motionless in her hospital bed. Evie was fifteen years old and already a seasoned veteran at fighting bone cancer, which rendered her legs useless. "I'm so angry with God about having cancer, and now I'm worried he doesn't love me anymore. Has God rejected me? Will I still go to heaven?"

At that point, she knew she was not much longer for this world. Heaven did await despite her fears. The sweet nectar of the gospel was spoken to her as she was reminded of God's active participation in her sufferings and his blessed promise to save. Nothing was more vivid for her than receiving into her mouth Christ's Holy Communion for just the second time in her short life—the first being her confirmation just weeks prior. She could taste with her tongue and with her faith that God is good (Ps 34:8). She directly encountered her Savior who suffered for her. God showed Evie just how much he still loves her, despite great fear brought on by the misbelief that God had rejected her. The gospel was mercy in action—the assurance of heaven to come for a young girl amid more suffering than many of us could ever imagine.

Evie went to heaven the next day. I can't wait to see her again in the resurrection.

For the sick and dying, suffering cannot be avoided. Therefore, the problem of suffering must be rightly understood in order to treat the soul properly. Unfortunately, the existence of suffering has often been regarded as the absence of God's favor. If suffering is present, then God isn't. For that reason, people are taught to avoid suffering whenever possible, ignore it, and even deny it since only pain comes with suffering and there is nothing positive attributed to it.

Suffering is not a mark to be avoided. In reality, it's an honest expression of God's will, hidden to our understanding as it might be. "But rejoice insofar as you share Christ's sufferings, that you may also rejoice and be glad when his glory is revealed" (1 Pet 4:13). It is not to be relegated to the sidelines of faith and life, nor does it indicate God's loss of favor or control. Suffering is an ever-present reality, not a mirage, but a lived-in experience that severely inflicts the human condition.

Suffering is a problem that stems from a common source—sin, the fallen world, and the devil. Because the source remains, the problem of suffering cannot be solved. Of course, finding a remedy to the problem means there is no longer a problem. Yet, in reality, suffering is an unsolvable problem to which there is no alternative other than to endure it and persevere under its effects. This is the realm in which pastors encounter the sick and dying. Pastors have no other alternative than to meet suffering head-on in the lives of others. The reality of suffering must be addressed. We are not called to solve the problem of suffering but treat it at its source and tend to its ugly effects. We can't explain it; we listen to it.

So, What Can Pastors Do?

First, the pastor needs to assess the condition of the soul. What causes the soul distress? Is the problem the result of unbelief or misbelief? What truths about the sick or dying person are known? Are they baptized? Are they confident of Christ's forgiveness for them? After careful exploration of needs, the physician of souls has a foundation for building a proper cure.

For the sick and dying, deep spiritual scars inflicted by sins committed or sins suffered at the hands of others rise to the surface and bring about great fear and distress. These times make souls feel a profound separation from God's favor as loneliness and isolation may consume them. Some distressed souls have a baptismal faith but also live in the far county, like the prodigal who wasted his father's inheritance in reckless living (Luke 15:11–32). They need to be brought back into a relationship with a Savior who desires to live in close proximity through the word and means of grace.

Visitation with pastoral care meets the soul where it is but does not leave it there. As the pastor reconnects the suffering soul to the life of Christ in the cross—the very picture of suffering—the salve of God's abundant comfort will flow through his life-giving word and the sacraments. There is no other foundation for a proper cure than that which the soul believes: God's word and the means of grace. For this reason, the narrative of Christ must come directly into the narrative of the sufferer—his sufferings applied to ours, not as a Band-Aid but rather as the soul's medicine, which comes through a Savior and goes right to the heart of the matter.

As the pastor listens to the story of the sufferer, the symptoms of the sin-sick soul emerge. The pastor interprets the symptoms in terms of what they disclose about the sufferer's relationship with God. The pastor dares not treat only the emotions of the sufferer, but rather the person as a whole. Often the sick and dying express a lack of patience toward God or rejection of God's will. Such expressions are symptoms of suffering and not the root cause.

Note that the distressed soul is never removed from Christ's identity as a fellow sufferer. Even more, the Christian life signifies total dependence on the Lord when it comes to obtaining what is needed for salvation. Since God hides in the midst of suffering, gospel proclamation and the sacraments are tailor-made for effective and intentional care. Jesus does not merely walk alongside sufferers; rather, he makes himself known to them and enters into their despair. We depend entirely on the Son of Man to treat the entirety of the person.

The cross of Christ reveals the reality hidden by sin that God is who he says he is in his word, in his works, and in his ways. Through his incarnation and suffering, God stands with us while our suffering is taking place. The mercy of the cross is joined with our most significant needs of forgiveness and freedom from sin, acceptance, and reconciliation. Through the cross, the Lord instills hope for a lost people. He grants help to the lonely. He embodies the true substance of the gospel for the indignant heart that cries out for God's relief. That relief is hidden in the pain and suffering of a Savior who knows the deep agony of carrying out the ultimate Christian vocation. Informed pastoral care and the application through visitation not only aims to comfort those who know all too well the emotional and spiritual trials created by sin, the devil, and the fallen world, but also demonstrates that they have not lost their position as precious and eternally kept creatures of God.

Selected Psalms, Readings, and Hymns for
Visitation to the Suffering and Despairing

➤ Psalms

Psalm 13, I have trusted in your steadfast
love

Psalm 34, When the righteous cry, the Lord
hears

Psalm 116, When I was brought low, he
saved me

Psalm 118, I shall not die, but I shall live

Psalm 130, Lord, hear my cry for mercy

Psalm 143, Answer me quickly, O Lord

➤ Readings

Job 42:1–6, God's purposes are supreme

Matthew 11:25–30, Jesus promises rest

John 5:24–29, The dead will hear and live

1 Thessalonians 4:13–18, We grieve in hope

➤ Hymns

Be Still, My Soul," Catharina Amalia
Dorothea von Schlegel

"Precious Lord, Take My Hand," Thomas
   A. Dorsey

"Jesus Christ, My Sure Defense," Otto von
   Schwerin

"In God, My Faithful God," Sigismund
   Weingärtner

Situation 2: Visitation before Surgery (Fear and Anxiety)

People often experience some level of anxiety before surgery. Ahead of them is the unknown. Will this surgery be successful and help me feel better? Will recovery be painful, and how long will it take? What if the worst thing imaginable happens and something goes wrong? Those preparing for surgery, no matter how routine or invasive, worry about themselves and those who depend on them.

One thing that often goes unnoticed is the anxiety and concern of those who care deeply about the patient. Pastors should take notice and address their spiritual needs during these times as well. The family will often act strong for the sake of the patient. They will speak confident words of comfort to ease worry. However, family and loved ones are often inflicted with anxious hearts as they silently worry over the outcome.

Paul's concluding remarks to the Philippians help us here. "Rejoice in the Lord always; again I will say, rejoice. Let your *reasonableness* be known to everyone. The Lord is at hand; *do not be anxious about anything, but in everything by prayer and supplication with thanksgiving let your requests be made known to God.* And the peace of God, which surpasses all understanding, will guard your hearts and minds in Christ Jesus" (Phil 4:4–7).

Anxiety is heightened when it is experienced alone. It is compounded when there is no room to rejoice. Paul tells us that there is always a time to rejoice. And, because our Lord is at hand, our reasonableness is attained and on display for others. The word Paul uses here includes the meanings "yielding, gentle, or courteous." These definitions point to the condition of the self. In anxious times, because the Lord is at hand, we yield with gentle courteousness and rejoice. God graciously remains with those who carry anxious hearts.

Paul says, "Do not be anxious," and then shares the alternative: "but in everything … let your requests be made known to God." Anxious hearts are not left alone. And what is more, God doesn't merely come to be present with the anxious. He comes to *give*. Peace is delivered amid fear. God's peace pierces into our hearts and souls beyond the mind (it surpasses all understanding!) and will protect the anxious. God's presence is not a passive standing beside those who worry but rather is active to bring peace amid tribulation.

So, What Can Pastors Do?

Pastoral visitation during times of surgery becomes the mechanism through which God delivers peace. Visit individuals and close family before the procedure occurs—either the night before or the morning before the surgery. If at all possible, remain with the family during the surgery. Your presence is more than just a comforting gesture or activity that members have come to expect. Pastors who visit are deliverers of God's promise. Pastors have a good word to share because it's a word that belongs to the almighty. Pastors are more than just a comforting presence but are instead stand-ins for God. They are instruments that deliver everything needful for anxious hearts going into surgery.

Jonathan was being prepped for open-heart surgery when I visited him at the hospital. He was convinced he was not going to survive. "Pastor, I'm scared. What if I don't make it and my family is left to fend for themselves without me?" It's no secret that fear is compounded when those experiencing it have loved ones who depend on them—especially when it's a matter of life or death.

We took up Philippians chapter 4 together. After reading the passage, I told him, "When Paul says, 'do not be anxious,' what he means is that we have no reason to be. The reason is because the peace of God passes our understanding and remains with us now and forever. No matter what, God's peace is ours."

We finished by praying, "Wait for the LORD; be strong, and let your heart take courage; wait for the LORD!" (Ps 27:14). We also prayed for the surgical team and his family. I gave him a blessing, "The Lord bless you and keep you and give you his PEACE," as he was taken back to the operating room. Jonathan took a deep breath and calmly nodded at me with thanks. I spent the rest of the morning in the waiting room with the family.

Notice that Paul does not tell the Philippians that anxiety will disappear when God delivers peace. Fallen human hearts still cling to uncertainties. The devil knows all too well how to sow seeds of doubt that divert eyes away from God's promises. Therefore, it is prudent for pastors to share diligently words of comfort that come from holy Scripture. Hold up the patient in prayer by asking God to send his strength, comfort, and peace. Include the loved ones in these prayers and, if possible and when appropriate, celebrate the Lord's Supper prior to surgery. Communion is another avenue by which God delivers his grace to anxious hearts.

Perhaps it is helpful to think of visitation as not so much the attempt to take something away as it is the opportunity to give something that God wants others to have. Paul's explicit message to the Philippians is precisely that. He doesn't mention taking away anxiety but rather giving peace. God's peace drives out anxiety. That's what pastors are called to do in proximity of those who need God's peace delivered to them. Pastoral visitation is a delivery vocation—especially to anxious hearts preparing for surgery or whatever the situation.

Selected Psalms, Readings, and Hymns for Visitation to the Fearful and Anxious

> Psalms

Psalm 4, The Lord alone makes me dwell in safety

Psalm 23, I will fear no evil, for you are with me

Psalm 46, God is our refuge and strength

Psalm 56, In God I trust; I shall not be afraid

Psalm 94, The Lord will not forsake his people

➤ Readings

Isaiah 35:3–10, God saves those with an anxious heart

Matthew 6:25–34, Seek first the kingdom of God

Romans 8:28–39, If God is for us, who can be against us?

Philippians 4:4–7, Do not be anxious about anything

1 Peter 5:6–11, Cast all your anxieties on him

➤ Hymns

"Lord, Take My Hand and Lead Me," Julie von Hausmann

"Have No Fear, Little Flock," Heinz Werner Zimmermann

"I Know My Faith Is Founded," Erdmann Neumeister

"Jesus, Savior, Pilot Me," Edward Hooper

SITUATION 3: VISITATION TO SHUT-INS (LONELY AND ISOLATED)

Visiting shut-ins is, for me, one of the most enjoyable parts of pastoral ministry. My doctoral thesis focused on improving soul care for this often less appreciated segment of both the church and society. As one might imagine, I discovered that loneliness and isolation from the family and church community were significant causes of spiritual despair.

Ida had recently lost her husband to a sudden heart attack. She was legally blind, had trouble walking, and depended on her husband to provide much of her daily care. Although she lived in a senior living facility with many neighbors close by, her husband's death resulted in a huge void in her life as now she was left without his steadfast care and companionship.

Loneliness due to her husband's death and isolation as a result of her disabilities filled Ida's heart with despair. When I visited her, she would question me about God's purpose for her life. Now that her husband was gone, she struggled with feeling that she was no longer a productive member of society. She saw herself as having little to no value in anyone's eyes. This once active member at our church felt as if her purpose for living—whether for her husband or for her Lord—did not exist any longer.

A misunderstood or underappreciated malady for seniors is the loss of vocation. Society relegates the aged to the sidelines by treating them as uneconomic burdens on valued resources—especially if they are plagued with disabilities. If the church is not careful, it too can act in this manner. The aged may feel this way about themselves as they realize they cannot serve their Lord as they once did. As a result, guilt may consume those who think their Christian identity has changed from valued producer for the sake of the church to burdensome consumer.

Shut-ins desire to maintain a link between the self and congregational life. Individuals gain a greater sense of identity by being a part of a greater whole. Pastoral visitation, then, acts as a conduit that supplies community connection to those who are unable to come to church. For this reason, the continuity of soul care through frequent visits is important. The more pastors and laity supply community to the homebound, the less isolated they become. When members cannot come to church, the church must go to them.

So, What Can Pastors Do?

A tactic that I employ quite often while visiting older adult shut-ins is called "life review," or as I call it, "self-narrative."[21] Allowing older adults to tell their stories often helps them to build a framework around their troubles where spiritual needs may be discovered and God's story applied. Telling one's story is fundamental to self-identity. Having a personal story is to have a sense of self and to lose the sense of the storyline of one's life is to lose the sense of being.[22] Stories help older adults find purpose and meaning by breaking down barriers of isolation and rediscovering their place among the history of others.

Older adults who make up the vast majority of shut-ins want to tell their story to recall and reclaim the past. Good and bad experiences are located in time. These stories mark a person's link to a greater narrative which forms the individual's identity before God and others. People don't just have memories of stories; these memories make them who they are.

Reviewing life's events helps older adults rediscover who they are and where they have been. Even more, it helps them realize that their Lord remains with them every step of the way. Instead of trying to escape loneliness, despair, and other challenges that shut-ins face, self-narrative helps them identify with the story of grace hidden in the suffering life of Jesus. Rather than turning away from their struggles, Christians need to explore self-narratives that place them in the midst of struggle and point them toward their Savior, who promises his eternal presence. The Christian story finds its true identity in a Savior who comes to embrace souls within the darkest of days, no matter how tragic the story.

Ida loved to tell me how she and her husband helped build the church they attended when they first got married. She loved to share stories about how her parents took in family members and cared for them when they were sick and in need. She boasted with pride over her children, the love of her husband, and her work at the church. As she told me these grand stories time after time, she rediscovered her place in the lives of others. She rediscovered within her personal discourse the places where God blessed her and others through her.

After a few months, Ida began to lead a Bible study at the senior living facility. It was geared to those who had trouble seeing and reading. She played the Bible on tape and talked about each passage. I sat with her during one of her studies. She told her stories. She shared God's word. Ida was an instrument of God with purpose.

Engaging shut-ins in telling their stories helps them connect to what they are still a part of even if they don't feel it—the church and their Lord. Pastors can help shut-ins rediscover their story within the story of Christ by listening and explaining how God provided care and love no matter what the situation. Those isolated from others are never without Jesus. He reminds us, "I am with you always, to the end of the age" (Matt 28:20).

For this reason, every story is a story of God's providence and care. Every story includes the story of how Jesus comes to give comfort and maintain an identity as one purchased through death on a cross.

Connecting the stories of shut-ins to the story of Christ helps those who are separated from the body of Christ rediscover that their identity remains affixed to Christ and his family. Pastoral visitation breaks into loneliness and isolation not only through the presence of the pastor, but also through the knowledge and comfort that they still belong to the community of believers.

Selected Psalms, Readings, and Hymns
for Visitation to the Lonely and Isolated

> Psalms

Psalm 16, The Lord will not abandon my soul

Psalm 38, Loneliness of being a sinner

Psalm 68, Father of the fatherless and protector of widows

Psalm 88, My soul is full of troubles; hear my cry

Psalm 142, When my spirit faints, you know my way

> Readings

Isaiah 49:13–16a, The Lord will not forget you

John 14:16–21, The Lord will not leave you as orphans

Romans 8:28–39, If God is for us, who can be against us?

2 Timothy 4:16–18, Paul deserted by all except the Lord

Hebrews 13:5, Be content; I will never leave you

> Hymns

"Why Should Cross and Trial Grieve Me," Paul Gerhardt

"The Lord's My Shepherd, I'll Not Want," The Psalms of David in Meeter (Edinburgh, 1650)

"If God Himself Be for Me," Paul Gerhardt

SITUATION 4: VISITATION TO THE LOST (UNBELIEF AND MISBELIEF)

Visitation to the complacent, the inactive, or those who have grown cold toward the church is no easy task. Pastors may think of it as one of the most distasteful duties. Pastors fear confrontation, like most everyone else. We may wrongly believe that delinquency is a glaring indictment that announces rejection of our ministry. Pastoral pride, the idea that it's our fault for the way we feel, may get in the way of seeking after the lost. There are many excuses that pastors may conjure up to ignore this important work.

Those who set themselves apart from Christ and the church put themselves in a dangerous—dare I say *deadly*—position. Ignoring the community of faith that gathers to receive the forgiveness of sins—that unites to build one another up—is spiritually damaging although not understood as such by the delinquent. They need visitation to show what they desperately need and to sound the alarm that their spiritual well-being is in grave danger. They need to hear God's law spoken directly to them so they understand the error of their ways.

Pastors can expect to encounter runaway members that must be retrieved. The perpetual work of patiently seeking after them will only come to an end on the last day. The Bible tells us, "All we like sheep have gone astray; we have turned—every one—to his own way" (Isa 53:6). So, God calls the wayward back to the fold, "Return, ye backsliding children, and I will heal your backslidings" (Jer 2:33 KJV). Apart from the Good Shepherd and his means of grace that sustain sinners, the sheep risk deadly attack. God desires to reestablish a relationship with the lost and provide the means of life they cannot obtain separated from him. He knows his sheep need him and each other. Pastors visit to address spiritual needs, such as unbelief that may consume their hearts or the misbelief that they do not need what God offers within the church.

So, What Can Pastors Do?

You may have heard it said, "Preach the gospel at all times. When necessary, use words." This quote is often attributed to Francis of Assisi. It is likely, though, he never spoke these words. The story of the pastor who visited the man by the fire is one example of how this saying is true. However, pastors should expect two things concerning pastoral care to the lost: the very act of visitation has meaning to the lost or straying, and words will be necessary.

The Bible is full of stories about the faithful running away and God seeking after them. Jesus's parable about leaving the ninety-nine to go find the one lost sheep is predicated upon actual circumstances that feature some of the Bible's most notable characters (Matt 18). They were part of the flock but then strayed from the fold. From Adam and Eve in the garden (Gen 3), to the children of Israel in the desert (Exod 16), and to Peter in the courtyard (Matt 26, Mark 14, Luke 22, John 18), pride and the devil's schemes veered even the most faithful away from the loving arms of the Good Shepherd. They became lost and vulnerable.

Like the examples in the Bible, misbelief is the malady pastors will encounter most with those who have strayed from church. Take, for example, Jesus visiting Nicodemus (John 3) or the Samaritan woman at the well (John 4). They needed to be gently directed away from their false ideas about religion and brought back to the truth. Jesus used visitation and words to accomplish this task. So do those called to seek after them. Pastors visit to bring the truth to bear on the souls of the wayward. This should be done with gentleness and in good order. The law is shared with all love and sincerity to win back the lost. The gospel is proclaimed to show how God loves them and gives them all they need for life and salvation.

Grace stopped attending church with her husband, Jordan. I visited their home one evening with the intent of discovering why and to invite her return. She told me that she didn't much like the liturgy and the hymns we sang. They seemed strange to her, she said, and she found very little within them that made her feel happy about church and God.

We took a little time to discuss why stirring up good feelings is not the main objective in worship. The most important part of worship is how our Lord comes to serve those who gather, how God's word of law convicts us of our sins, and how the gospel explicitly shows his love for us. I took time to listen to her reasons and respond with gentle guidance while helping her to realize that I understood her hang-ups.

Grace suffered from misbelief concerning the purpose of worship. I recommended that she try attending church with Jordan again, and, instead of thinking about feelings, focus on God's word of promise for her. Instead of gauging worship's value in terms of emotion, look for all the times God shares with her what she needs—forgiveness and salvation.

Notice that I did not explicitly tell Grace that she was sinning because of her overt disregard for worship. Notice that I never spoke the command, "Remember the Sabbath day, to keep it holy" (Exod 20:8). Sometimes it is true, the pastor's very presence can speak God's law without using words. She knew why I was there. If she didn't, I would have the responsibility to make that clear. So, instead of pounding her with the law, I used words of encouragement to help her realize the blessings she was missing. By addressing her misbelief with the gospel, she now understood the purpose and importance of being in the Lord's house. It was not to make her feel good. It was for a far more meaningful and gracious reason.

I am thankful that she did return to church and became a regular attendee with her husband. The conversation that led her to realize the church's value would have never happened if I had not been intentional about visiting her. My approach to this situation showed her that I was genuinely concerned about her absence rather than eager to condemn her. It was important that I got to know her, which opened the door for my direct question about her absence. Our honest conversation informed me of what she needed and led her to give church another try. Now, she receives the means of grace with her fellow believers quite regularly. Now, she and her husband have children of their own who remain an active part of the church community.

Selected Psalms, Readings, and Hymns for Visitation to those with Misbelief or Unbelief

> Psalms

Psalm 1, The way of the righteous

Psalm 25, The Lord instructs sinners in the way

Psalm 43, Let your light and truth lead me

Psalm 53, The fool says there is no God

Psalm 119:41–48, I will speak of your testimonies

Psalm 115, Not to us, but to your name give glory

> Readings

Ezekiel 34:11–34, The Lord will search for his sheep

John 6:66–69, Jesus has the words of eternal life

Acts 4:12, There is salvation in Jesus alone

1 Timothy 6:3–12, Take hold of eternal life

> Hymns

"Jesus Sinners Doth Receive," Erdmann Neumeister

"The King of Love My Shepherd Is," Henry W. Baker

"Christ, the Word of God Incarnate," Steven P. Mueller

"Lord, Keep us Steadfast in Your Word," Martin Luther

Situation 5: Visitation Amid Tragedy (Grief and Shame)

My phone rang at 3 a.m. waking me from a deep sleep. I answered, expecting the worst as is usually the case at such an hour, and the worst came to pass. It was Colleen, a single mother with a son who was a corporal in the Marine Corp. She said through her tears, "Pastor, sorry to wake you, but I just received word that my son, Matthew, was killed in Afghanistan."

Matthew was on his third tour of duty. He wasn't required to accept this assignment but volunteered because he was, as he put it, young and single. He didn't think it was a good idea for married men with children to be on the front lines putting themselves in harm's way. His mother was not fond of his decision but respected it. Matthew was that kind of person. He put country and others first.

I arrived at Colleen's house not long afterward. Her mother and father were already there grieving with her. As we embraced, she said to me, "Pastor, I should have never let him go back. I should have talked him out of it. I feel so guilty." This misguided feeling added fuel to her grief. She was not at fault, but no one at the time could tell her differently.

Colleen felt guilt, but she was not guilty. Guilt is an objective state. It means that a person did something wrong and now possesses this condition. But Colleen did nothing wrong in this situation. Instead, she was experiencing shame, which is often confused with guilt. Guilt is sin committed; shame is sin suffered.[23] She suffered shame due to her son's death, a death she had nothing to do with.

When grief comes to bear on the hearts of the bereaved, oftentimes they will find a way to blame themselves. They feel guilty or, rightly put, feel ashamed of what they did or did not do to prevent this horrible experience. This is particularly dangerous when tragedy strikes because shame has people hiding away from God rather than moving toward him. The psalmist reminds us, "He will cover you with his pinions, and under his wings you will find refuge; his faithfulness is a shield and buckler" (Ps 91:4). Yet, shame drives them away from his company rather than leading them to seek refuge within it. Grief and shame strip the despairing soul bare by exposing its nakedness. It robs souls of God's glory and burdens them with feelings of emptiness and regret. When souls are already crushed by grief because of tragedy, only the presence of God and his promise of peace can bring comfort and relief.

Grief comes when we are separated from someone or something we love. It's the hurt and emptiness felt due to something that was once whole and is now fragmented. Grief is a response to loss. We have all felt this feeling at one time or another. We know the brokenness of losing something or someone that we hoped never to be without.

Our Lord knows this type of grief. He sorrowed over the broken relationships he had with his people before destroying the world in the great flood, save Noah and his family (Gen 6:9–22). We hear how Jesus grieved over John the Baptizer's death (Matt 14:1–12) and how he wept over his friend, Lazarus (John 11:1–16). The Bible clearly shows how grief is not at odds with faith or contrary to the gospel. Instead, grief exists alongside faith and the gospel just as God's goodness remains intact while he himself experienced tragedy. "Blessed are those who mourn, for they shall be comforted" (Matt 5:4).

So, What Can Pastors Do?

Tragedy beckons the need for intentional pastoral care that actively moves toward the disheartened.

In fact, with tragedy, visitation should be an immediate response. I didn't wait to see Colleen and her family. I got up that very moment and headed over to her house. Grief hits hard from the start, and the initial impact is harsh. Pastoral care cannot wait. I knew my job was to be there—to listen, provide comfort, pray, and bless.

When a tragedy has taken place, pastors will often find grieving individuals confused and in shock. They aren't sure how to process what happened and may be quite anxious about what comes next. They aren't sure how to live with a heart now torn apart as they become more and more afraid of what life will now be like.

The Swiss-American psychiatrist Elizabeth Kübler-Ross famously described the five general stages of grief: denial, anger, bargaining, depression, and acceptance. While it is popular to think of these stages as a process, Kübler-Ross said they are not meant to be neatly packaged up steps. There is no typical grief because it is an individual and not a linear process.[24] And all five stages are not necessarily experienced by any one individual. Pastors can expect those they visit to exhibit any number of these stages at any time.

Pastoral care for those who experience tragedy is a "with" journey. It is described as a journey because it has a definite course. Pastors will need to continue to actively visit those who experience grief as they attempt to navigate through the roller-coaster of emotions and spiritual challenges. There is no timetable for grief, nor should pastors impose one. Grief can cause any number of encumbrances to spiritual well-being, so pastors should keep a sharp eye out for what troubles the soul each time they visit. Because shame—masquerading as guilt—is often attached to grief, those who are thrown into its clutches will often segment themselves away from the body of Christ. They will grieve in solitude with anger directed toward God or perhaps feel that their actions caused his wrathful spite. They will perhaps fear facing God or those within the community of believers who desire to support them. Grief will drive sufferers toward isolation, which will inevitably negatively affect their spiritual well-being.

Visitation puts the pastor alongside the bereaved to provide God's comfort. The continuity of care provided through intentional visitation demonstrates to the bereaved that the pastor is not a reluctant traveler along this journey but a willing companion. The objective is not to take away grief but rather to enter into it by walking alongside the bereaved. So, the pastor comes beside the bereaved with a listening ear that serves as a constant reminder that their shepherd remains along for the ride.

Grief is not a puzzle to be solved but rather a present reality that must take its course. There are no shortcuts through grief. If the objective is somehow to eliminate it, pastors will tend to focus only on its outward expressions and not treat the central maladies of the soul. The Bible does not show us an explicit remedy to grief. Instead, it demonstrates how God remains with the bereaved with promises of comfort and peace. This, then, is the shepherd's job. The pastor should remain with the bereaved as well.

Kenneth Haugk, founder of *Stephen Ministries*, authored a four-part series of books called Journeying through Grief. These books help the bereaved navigate many of the emotions they will experience through the various stages. I have found the stories and biblical content are helpful conversation starters that open up avenues for the bereaved to tell their own stories. Here is how I use these books when I visit the bereaved.

A week after the funeral, I will visit the bereaved and give them the first book in the series. I ask that they read the book, and then I will visit a few weeks later to discuss it. The books come alongside the reader in their grief journey through relational stories and helpful insights. They include biblical truths about grief that give a clearer picture of what sufferers may expect.[25] These books do a good job of framing grief in a way that is helpful to the bereaved.

During the second visit, I give them the second book with the intention of visiting a couple of months later to discuss it. During the third visit, I give them the third book and visit a couple of months after that. Finally, I give them the fourth book and plan to visit on the one-year anniversary of the tragedy. I have often found that this milestone visit is the most difficult for the bereaved. They may have certain expectations about how far along in the grief process they should be, and yet they may still feel consumed by grief. Continuing care is necessary, along with reminders that there are no timetables for grief and that there is nothing abnormal about experiencing deep grief.

All in all, five separate visits are made within a year. Of course, each situation varies, and so does the necessity for visitation. At the conclusion of each visit, the pastor and the bereaved may want to celebrate Holy Communion—the means of grace that unites the grieving member to the church (both the living and those already in heaven) and the Lord through the power of forgiveness. The sacrament embodies the purpose of pastoral care through visitation—reconciliation to God and the clear testimony that the bereaved are not apart from but a part of Christ's church.

Grief brings disorder and chaos to those who experience it. The soul is left in turmoil, often wondering how life will go on or if some semblance of normal will ever return. The truth is, the bereaved will have to accept a new normal. The goal throughout this journey is to bring order and reconciliation to the soul amid the new normal for life as they know it. God's word and his ever-present blessing and hope is placed before them through the ministers who are called to bring it. Pastoral visitation plays a crucial role in the process of grief.

Selected Psalms, Readings, and Hymns for Visitation to those with Grief and Shame

➢ Psalms

Psalm 6, The Lord has heard my plea

Psalm 25, Let me not be put to shame

Psalm 32, I confessed my sin, and you forgave

Psalm 51, Create in me a clean heart

Psalm 102, The Lord regards the prayer of the destitute

➢ Readings

Genesis 3:1–15, 21, Adam's shame and God's first promise

Isaiah 43:10–13, Fear not; the Lord helps you

John 3:14–21, God sent his Son to save the world

Colossians 1:19–23, Through Christ God reconciled to himself all things

1 John 2:28, Believers will not shrink from Christ in shame

> Hymns

"Jesus Sinners Doth Receive," Erdmann
  Neumeister

"Baptismal Waters Cover Me," Kurt E.
  Reinhard

"From Depths of Woe I Cry to Thee,"
  Martin Luther

"Jesus, Thy Blood and Righteousness,"
  Nicolaus Ludwig von Zinzendorf

"Jesus, Priceless Treasure," Johann Franck

Conclusion

God calls pastors to enter into the lives of those
they serve. Visitation is the active embodiment of
how this occurs within the extraordinary circumstances of people who need personalized soul care.
This is a "with" journey—and it cannot take place
from a distance. The shepherd tends the sheep in
the same field where they eat and sleep.

Yet, pastors cannot do it all. Pastors need to
understand when needs go beyond what they can
provide. Referrals to skilled professionals who can
provide mental and emotional care are not only
prudent but sometimes necessary. Pastors should

have a list of trusted professionals who provide counseling services. When referrals take place, pastors should not think they can now forfeit the continuum of soul care. Instead, they should think of counseling as care that comes alongside of essential soul care that should remain persistent.

Pastors cannot do it all. The church community often provides much-needed and effective support in times of need. Calling elders may provide another ear to listen to. Care groups within the church family can arrange for food deliveries or transportation needs. While the pastor may be the person most aware of important needs, he cannot provide for all of them alone. Delegating responsibilities helps pastors budget their precious time and gives others the opportunity to carry out their Christian vocation for others.

The situations described in this chapter need a visiting pastor. Of course, there are many other situations not mentioned here that need the same. However, in each of these situations, the pastor was not alone. Whether it be assistance from members within the church or neighbors in the community, care and comfort is brought to the lost and afflicted. Visitation is individualistic and personal but not an isolated endeavor. When members grieve, the whole community of faith is involved providing comfort to the lost and care for the brokenhearted. "If one member suffers, all suffer together; if one member is honored, all rejoice together" (1 Cor 12:26).

CHAPTER 7

Word of Encouragement

*"I was sick and you visited me, I was in prison
and you came to me."*

IN JESUS'S NARRATIVE ABOUT THE FINAL JUDG-
ment, the ones he called righteous had no idea
what he was talking about. We can imagine them
looking quizzically at one another and compelled
to ask a clarifying question, "And when did we see
you sick or in prison and visit you?"

Jesus, confident and resolute, responds, "Truly,
I say to you, as you did it to one of the least of
these my brothers, you did it to me" (Matt 25:36,
39, 40).

Visitors visit Jesus. That's right, I know it's difficult sometimes to see Jesus in the broken bodies
of the sick, the defiant faces of the obstinate, or the

quaking hearts of the suffering. I realize that scandals revealed by sinners and despair verbalized by souls wrought with fear dull our view of the perfect Savior within others. But, dear brothers and sisters in Christ, it is true. You visit Jesus, just like he says in the Gospel of Matthew.

We visit Jesus because Jesus is with those we visit. And, thank God for that. There is no way we could do it without him. There is no way those we visit could either. Knowing that we are never alone is the true comfort on which all of us depend. We could never do it alone. We are never alone.

Isn't it beautiful and heartening? Jesus leaves us with that very promise at the end of the Gospel of Matthew, "I am with you always, to the end of the age" (Matt 28:20). Jesus left that place; he left and ascended into heaven, but his promise holds true. He did remain with them—and with us—forever.

Jesus told the disciples at that Great Commission to go and make disciples. In other words, make *more* disciples than just you, by baptizing and teaching. There is no way this could be done without Jesus present with them. He comes near those he loves. He loves those he baptizes and teaches. Through his word and sacrament, Jesus visits his people.

Visitation puts visitors in close and intimate proximity to Jesus. Visitation puts those who are visited in close and intimate proximity with Jesus. This is the whole point.

Where Jesus is, comfort is received.

Where Jesus is, wounds are healed.

Where Jesus is, sins are forgiven.

Visitors bring Jesus. Visitors make known the active power of God's love that desires to come into our midst and meet us where we are.

We dare not take for granted the blessed privilege it is to be a pastor who is called by God to visit his precious loved ones. Yes, visitation is hard, time-consuming work. Yes, it takes a lot of patience and planning. Yes, it takes experience to become good at it. You are his chosen instrument, God's foot soldier, made ready to do battle against sin, death, and the devil. He chose you.

Be not discouraged by its challenges. Visitations rarely go perfectly. Some go nothing like what was intended. This is the reality of ministry and, at times, it is quite messy. Please take it as it comes. Know that the Lord is with you every step of the way. You will struggle. Know that when you do, you are in good company with the holy apostles of yesterday, today, and tomorrow. There will be times when you will need to step back, catch your breath, and take a break. Do so for your own sake, recharge your spiritual batteries, and then get back to it when you are ready. Every pastor has struggled in their hearts and minds because of visitation—even Jesus himself.

Take courage, beloved in the Lord. Remember, you are never alone. You visit Jesus. You visit others *with* Jesus at your side and on your lips. And, most assuredly, Jesus visits you with his promise that he will not leave you nor forsake you (Deut 31:8). He grants strength and comfort to visitors because you embark on his holy mission—the divine work of caring for those entrusted to you within unique, challenging, and unpredictable circumstances. Visitation is God's holy work indeed.

God—Father, Son, and Holy Spirit—bless you and keep you. God grant you his unending strength. Amen.

Appendix

A Brief Service of the Word for
Use during Pastoral Visitation

Throughout the church's history, rites and services based on God's word were created for different pastoral care situations. Below is a basic Service of the Word that can be modified and used to fit within a variety of visitation contexts. Other psalms, readings, and prayers may be added. This brief service could also be used alongside the service of the sacrament if Holy Communion is celebrated. The pastor begins by speaking the parts in regular type while the individual or individuals respond by speaking the words in bold font.

Invocation

In the name of the Father, Son, and Holy Spirit.
Amen.

O Lord, open my lips,

And my mouth will declare your praise. *Ps 51:15*

Make haste, O God, to deliver me!

O Lord, make haste to help me! *Ps 70:1*

Psalmody

In you, O Lord, do I take refuge;

Let me never be put to shame;

In your righteousness deliver me!

Incline your ear to me;

Rescue me speedily!

Be a rock of refuge for me,

A strong fortress to save me!

For you are my rock and my fortress;

And for your name's sake you lead me
and guide me;

You take me out of the net they have
hidden for me,

For you are my refuge.

Into your hand I commit my spirit;

You have redeemed me, O Lord,
faithful God. *Ps 31:1–5*

Glory be to the Father and to the Son and the
Holy Spirit; as it was in the beginning, is
now, and will be forever. Amen.

Reading from Holy Scripture

A reading from _____, chapter _____.

This is the word of the Lord.
Thanks be to God.

Sermon or Meditation

Select a hymn appropriate to the situation of the visit. Here a few suggestions.

➢ Time of Illness

"I Lay My Sins on Jesus," Horatius Bonar

"Your Hand, O Lord, in Days of Old," Edward H. Plumptre (English adapt. Ralph Williams)

"How Firm a Foundation," A selection of Hymns, London, 1787

"When to Our World the Savior Came," Timothy Dudley-Smith

➢ Time of Death

"Lord, Thee I love with All My Heart," Martin Schalling; tr. Catherine Winkworth

"I walk in Danger All the Way," Hans Adolf Brorson; tr. Ditlef G. Ristad

"Let Us Ever Walk with Jesus," Sigismund von Birken

"Abide with Me," Henry F. Lyte

> Time of Distress

"Lord, Take My Hand and Lead Me," Julie von Hausmann

"A Mighty Fortress is Our God," Martin Luther

"Have No Fear, Little Flock," Heinz Werner Zimmermann

"Jesus, Savior Pilot Me," Edward Hopper

> Home and Family

"Father, All Creating," John Ellerton

"Lord Jesus Christ, the Children's Friend," Henry L. Lettermann

"Great Is Thy Faithfulness," Thomas O. Chisholm

"How Clear is Our Vocation, Lord," Fred Pratt Green

"The Lord's My Shepherd, I'll Not Want," The Psalms of David in Meeter, Edinburgh, 1650

➢ Time of Celebration

"My Soul, Now Praise Your Maker," Johann
Gramann

"From All That Dwell Below the Skies,"
Isaac Watts

"Now Thank We All Our God," Martin
Rinckart; tr. Catherine Winkworth

"Bless the Lord, My Soul," Isaac Watts

"What God Ordains Is Always Good,"
Samuel Rodigast

PRAYER

The Lord be with you
And with your spirit. *2 Tim 4:22*

Let us pray:

Visit, O Lord, the homes in which Your people dwell,
and keep all harm and danger far from them. Grant
that we may dwell together in peace under the protection of Your holy angels, sharing eternally in your
blessings; through Jesus Christ, our Lord.[26]
Amen.

› If time allows, offer a prayer specific to the situation of the visit, whether *ex corde* or out of a prayer book.[27]

Almighty God, we give you most humble and hearty thanks for all your goodness and loving-kindness to us and to all people.

We praise you for our creation, preservation, and all the blessings of this life, but above all for the inestimable love in the redemption of the world by our Lord and Savior Jesus Christ, for the means of grace, and for the hope of glory.

We ask you to give us hearts for mercy and thanksgiving that we might show forth your praise with both our lips and our lives.

Sustain and comfort us in every time of trouble, and finally recieve us into your everlasting kingdom; through your infinite mercy in Christ Jesus our Savior who taught us to pray:[28]

Our Father who art in heaven
Hallowed be thy name,
Thy kingdom come,
Thy will be done on earth as it is in heaven;
Give us this day our daily bread;

**And forgive us our trespasses as we forgive
those who trespass against us;
And lead us not into temptation,
But deliver us from evil.
For thine is the kingdom and
the power and the glory
forever and ever. Amen.**   *Matt 6:9–13*

Let us bless the Lord:

Thanks be to God.

The almighty and merciful Lord, the Father, the Son, and the Holy Spirit, bless and keep you.

Amen.

Annotated Bibliography

BOOKS ABOUT VISITATION

> Banks, Bonny V. *Hospital Visitation Guide for Ministers*. Amherst, Ohio: Steward Publishing, 2011.

This book is a practical and comprehensive guide that touches on much of what a visitor should consider before and during a hospital visit. Banks covers general protocols to keep in mind, practical concerns during visits, and the care of souls for those under distress. She even covers matters pertaining to health insurance and considerations for do-not-resuscitate (DNR) agreements. Biblical texts are scattered throughout the book.

> Croft, Brian. *Visit the Sick: Ministering God's Grace in Times of Illness*. Grand Rapids: Zondervan, 2014.

Croft begins by exploring God's care for the sick found within the narratives of the Scriptures. He then builds on this foundation by showing how visitors can put the theological principles found in the Bible into motion. Most of the book focuses on practical implications with appropriate how-to suggestions. At the conclusion of the book, he illustrates how to build a community of caretakers for the sick from among the saints who serve others when illness strikes the body of Christ.

> Lyle, Bradford. *Building Relationships through Pastoral Visitation*. Pennsylvania: Judson, 1984.

This handy book is a short survey of why visitation remains an important endeavor within the church. Included is a chapter on listening, which provides valuable practical insights that visitors will find useful. The author also explores various kinds of visits that pastors and laypeople should consider. He ends with a short section on training laypeople to visit with helpful guidelines for what he calls friendly visits.

> Savage, H. E. *Pastoral Visitation*. 1905. Repr., Leopold Classic Library, 2015.

This early classic text may be mostly antiquated but is still worth considering. The section called "House to House Visiting" has much the pastor will want to consider—both practically and theologically. Savage covers topics as practical as what to talk about and what tone to use during the visit. He also expands theologically by addressing visitation as it relates to preaching. One will probably not find much help from outdated portions such as those labeled "Difficulty of Meeting Women" and "Difficulty of Long Streets." Although, some may find them amusing and nostalgic considering the day and age in which they were written.

> Stubblefield, Jerry M. *Serving in Church Visitation*. Grand Rapids: Zondervan, 2002.

Stubblefield writes for a broad audience that includes novice and experienced visitors alike. This book is written for group training and for individuals who want to sharpen visitation skills. The author illustrates the points of preparation and enactment in a very easy-to-understand way. Though the book is easy, it is not shallow. He covers a wide range of topics that are essential to know before embarking on a visitation ministry.

Resources for Visitation

> Bonar, Andrew A. *The Visitor's Book of Texts*. Carlisle, PA: Banner of Truth Trust, 2010.

Bonar writes this resource based on the premise that the sick is best served through the simplest forms of scriptural truth. There are three parts divided into categories that address the sick and the sorrowful. Each section includes suggested passages with brief words of commentary scattered throughout.

> Cobb, David, and Derek Olsen, eds. *St. Augustine's Prayer Book*. Cincinnati: Forward Movement, 2014.

This short book is designed to enhance the Christian life through the discipline of prayer and devotion. However, its prayers and litanies serve as valuable tools for individual pastoral care. Cobb, an Episcopal priest, mentions in the foreword that this prayer book is most useful as preparation for worship and is designed to address specific needs individuals may have.

> Flynn, Vinny, and Erin Flynn. *Mass and Adoration Companion*. Charlotte, NC: TAN Books, 2017.

This Roman Catholic companion volume includes prayers, rites, and liturgies perfect for pastoral care during visitation. Prayers are divided into occasions and make up a vast majority of the content.

➢ Just, Arthur A. Jr., and Scot A. Kinnaman, eds.
  Visitation: Resources for the Care of Souls. St.
  Louis: Concordia, 2008.

This robust resource has five distinct sections. The first section features twenty-eight bedside devotions. The next three sections target what Kinnaman calls spiritual and emotional topics. These sections include visitation devotions broken down by topic, scriptural resources, and prayers addressing specific situations. The last section comprises various rites such as Holy Baptism in an emergency situation and other occasional brief services of the word. Visitors will find this comprehensive resource to be a valued treasure for situational pastoral care.

➢ Lilienthal, Michael G. *Pastoral Visitation Diary.*
  Self-published, 2019 (https://www.lulu.com/
  spotlight/GoodPilgrim).

This is an excellent record-keeping resource that will help visitors stay organized. Lilienthal divides the diary into sections that include calendars for regular visits, forms for visitation and prayer requests, visit tracking outlines, and plenty of blank pages for notes. Also within this volume are situational hymns, selected psalms set to chant tones, and Scriptures.

> ❯ Mech, Timothy J. *Pastors and Elders: Caring for the Church and One Another*. St. Louis: Concordia, 2011.

This training manual includes videos, PowerPoint presentations, and handouts that assist pastors and elders to understand and carry out their duties. The videos, in particular, help demonstrate various visitation scenarios that elders may encounter. The goal-setting promoted within the training encourages pastors and elders to plan and work together.

> ❯ Short, David, and David Searle. *Pastoral Visitation: A Pocket Manual*. Christian Focus, 2005.

This book is a collection of Scripture promises, prayers with prayer topic suggestions, and hymns for twenty different pastoral care situations divided up into chapters. Each chapter has a brief introduction for visitors to consider before entering the situation. After each Scripture, the authors write a brief word of encouragement based on each passage. There is also a hymn index and a subject index for quick referral.

Prayer Books and Hymnals

> Parish Priest, *A Manual of Pastoral Visitation: Intended for the Use of the Clergy in their Visitation of the Sick and Afflicted, 1868.* Repr., Kessinger, 2010.

This long-standing manual for the clergy was developed to be a comprehensive Book of Offices with Scriptures and prayers for pastoral visitation of the sick. The Offices are primarily composed of prayers and responses with detailed rubrics. The conclusion of the book has an extensive index of theological works, which include pertinent works of the church fathers, short sermons, devotional writings, and a list of prayers and Scriptures. Although this work has been around for more than a century and a half, users may find the various situational Offices useful.

> The Book of Common Prayer. *Various editions.*

The Book of Common Prayer has shaped the liturgical imagination of the church in the English-speaking world. As a Christian rule of life, it offers orders of service for prayer, Holy Communion, rites of life (like baptism, marriage, and death), as well as numerous prayers, a psalter, and a lectionary (a Bible-reading plan). Rites for healing are also included. These pastoral rites are comprised of a brief service of the word, a service of anointing, a service of Holy Communion, as well as many prayers—not only prayers to be prayed for the sick and dying but prayers to be prayed by the sick and dying.

But because there are an unusual number of editions of the Book of Common Prayer—5,000 in 200 languages—three should be especially noted:

- The prayer book of the Anglican Church North America (ACNA), *The Book of Common Prayer* (Anglican Liturgy Press, 2019)

- The prayer book of The Episcopal Church (TEC), *The Book of Common Prayer* (Church Publishing, 1979)

- The classic prayer book of 1662, available in many reprints, for example, *The 1662 Book of Common Prayer: International Edition*, eds. Samuel L. Bray and Drew Nathaniel Keane (IVP Academic, 2021)

The ACNA prayer book alone includes a Reconciliation of Penitents, which may prove helpful as you visit those estranged from church or under church discipline.

> *Evangelical Lutheran Worship: Pastoral Care.*
> Minneapolis: Augsburg Fortress, 2008.

This hymnal companion has a comprehensive section called, "Ministry in Sickness and Health" that is useful for visitors. Not only do the categories address spiritual and physical challenges, they also include unique circumstances for which pastors may need resources. More occasions are listed with accompanying readings and prayers toward the end of this volume.

> *Lutheran Book of Worship: Occasional Services.*
> Minneapolis: Augsburg, 1982.

This companion to the *Lutheran Book of Worship* (1978) includes occasional rites conveniently categorized for pastoral use. It also includes a section called, "Psalms, Lessons and Prayers" with headings for sixteen different care situations. Each section has a psalm, one or more Scripture lessons, and a prayer.

> *Lutheran Service Book: Pastoral Care Companion.*
> St. Louis: Concordia, 2007.

This is an Agenda companion to the *Lutheran Service Book* (2006), a hymnal produced by the Lutheran Church—Missouri Synod that contains occasional rites and services for congregational use. It also includes hymns and prayers that are chosen for appropriate pastoral care occasions. Its compact size makes it quite portable and ideal for use during visitation.

PASTORAL THEOLOGY

> ‣ Oden, Thomas C. *Pastoral Theology: Essentials of Ministry*. San Francisco: HarperCollins, 1983.

Oden includes a rather lengthy section dedicated to pastoral visitation that is mostly absent in other pastoral theology books. He addresses a broad range of topics, including encumbrances to visitation, visitation as exemplified by Jesus and the apostles, guidelines for visits, and a helpful practicum that aids visitors in considering personal and external factors that affect visitation.

> ‣ Warneck, Richard H. *Pastoral Ministry: Theology and Practice*. St. Louis: Concordia, 2018.

While this theology does not directly address the topic of pastoral visitation, the impetus of individual soul care exists throughout the entirety of the volume. This work is a foundational guide for the training of pastors and an essential resource for the continuum of growth in the realm of the care of souls.

Pastoral Care Resourses

> Eyer, Richard C. *Pastoral Care under the Cross: God in the Midst of Suffering.* St. Louis: Concordia, 2014.

Eyer writes from a hospital chaplain's perspective. He orients his book around what Martin Luther called "the theology of the cross," which is described as God's way of caring for his people through his own suffering. Particularly helpful for visitors is the section called "The Cross in Action: Practical Pastoral Care in Specific Circumstances." His sections on ministry to the elderly, the ill, and the dying build a strong foundation for visitors who will inevitably find themselves ministering to this segment of the congregation.

> Peterson, Eugene H. *Five Smooth Stones for Pastoral Work.* Grand Rapids: Eerdmans, 1980.

In this book, Peterson describes pastoral work framed within five books of the Old Testament—Song of Songs, Ruth, Lamentations, Ecclesiastes, and Esther. Chapter 2, called "Story-Making: Ruth," includes an insightful section on counseling and visitation. Peterson accentuates the advantages of modern visitation by calling its biblical use authentic pastoral acts. He also warns of the misunderstandings of visitation by explaining how God's word illustrates its improper use.

> ➢ Willimon, William H. *Worship as Pastoral Care.* Nashville: Abingdon, 1979.

This book's aim is to help readers understand how worship and pastoral care can inform, challenge, enrich, and support one another. Particularly helpful is chapter 2, which reminds pastors that worship has a caring dimension by which there is no true pastoral care apart from the worshiping, believing, and caring community of faith.

Works Cited

Bonhoeffer, Dietrich. *Spiritual Care*. Translated by Jay C. Rochelle. Fortress, 1985.

Bucer, Martin. *Concerning the True Care of Souls*. Translated by Peter Beale. Banner of Truth Trust, 2009.

Butler, Robert. "The Life Review: An Interpretation of Reminiscence in the Aged." *Psychiatry* 26, no. 1 (1963): 65–76.

Chambers, Oswald. *Workmen of God: The Cure of Souls*. Marshall, Morgan & Scott, 1937.

Gerkin, Charles V. *The Living Human Document: Re-Visioning Pastoral Counseling in a Hermeneutical Mode*. Abingdon, 1984.

"Global E-mail Spam Rate from 2012 to 2018," Joseph Johnson, *Statista*, https://www.statista.com/statistics/270899/global-e-mail-spam-rate/.

Harrison, Matthew C. *Letters from a Pastor's Heart*. Concordia, 2016.

"Journeying through Grief," *Stephen Ministries*, https://www.stephenministries.org/griefresources/default.cfm/774.

Just, Arthur A., Jr., *Heaven on Earth: The Gifts of Christ in the Divine Service*. Concordia, 2008.

Kleinig, John W. *Grace Upon Grace: Spirituality for Today*. Concordia, 2008.

Kleinig, John W. "Liturgy and the Delivery of a Good Conscience; Our Earthly Reception of Heavenly Gifts; Comfort, Comfort, Ye, My People." Paper presented at the Institute on Liturgy, Preaching and Church Music, Concordia University. Seward, NE. 28 July 2014.

Miller, Donald G. *Fire in Thy Mouth*. Baker, 1954.

Peterson, Eugene H. *Five Smooth Stones for Pastoral Work*. Eerdmans, 1980.

Peterson, Eugene H. *A Long Obedience in the Same Direction: Discipleship in an Instant Society*. InterVarsity Press, 1980.

Peterson, Eugene H. *The Pastor: A Memoir*. HarperOne, 2011.

Senkbeil, Harold L. *The Care of Souls: Cultivating a Pastor's Heart*. Lexham Press, 2019.

"Understanding Grief and Loss: An Overview," *HealGrief*, https://healgrief.org/understanding-grief/?gclid=EAIaIQobChMI5ei42qb-7gIVGuy1Ch14YwaSEAAYASAAEgKk_PD_BwE.

Notes

1. Range of usage—mustering of an army, census, to appoint to duty, divine judgment, including a few others.

2. Martin Bucer, *Concerning the True Care of Souls*, trans. Peter Beale (Banner of Truth Trust, 2009), 191.

3. Dietrich Bonhoeffer, *Spiritual Care*, trans. Jay C. Rochelle (Fortress, 1985), 45.

4. Also reference Matthew 25:34–36 to be reminded that when we visit Christ's people in their needs, we visit Jesus.

5. Donald G. Miller, *Fire in Thy Mouth* (Baker, 1954), 83.

6. Bucer, *Concerning the True Care of Souls*, 77.

7. Also very applicable to visitation are verses 1–3 of the same book and chapter: "Let brotherly love continue. Do not neglect to show hospitality to strangers, for thereby some have entertained angels unawares. Remember those who are in prison, as though in prison with them, and those who are mistreated, since you also are in the body."

8. John W. Kleinig, *Grace Upon Grace: Spirituality for Today* (Concordia, 2008), 283.

9. Arthur A. Just Jr., *Heaven on Earth: The Gifts of Christ in the Divine Service* (Concordia, 2008), 279.

10. Eugene H. Peterson, *Five Smooth Stones for Pastoral Work* (Eerdmans, 1980), 96.

11. Matthew C. Harrison, *Letters from a Pastor's Heart* (Concordia, 2016), 71.

12. Eugene H. Peterson, *The Pastor: A Memoir* (HarperOne, 2011), 86–87.

13. See the resources listed in the bibliography and the appendix.

14. I say, "general introductory portion of the conversation" because I find it too cumbersome to stop the conversation or introductory remarks and spell out some sort of purpose and then restart the conversation where it was before. Stating the purpose while in the midst of the conversation, for me, flows much nicer into various topics that you, either of you, might wish to discuss.

15. Harold L. Senkbeil, *The Care of Souls: Cultivating a Pastor's Heart* (Lexham Press, 2019), 100.

16. John W. Kleinig, "Liturgy and the Delivery of a Good Conscience; Our Earthly Reception of Heavenly Gifts; Comfort, Comfort, Ye, My People" (paper presented at the Institute on

Liturgy, Preaching and Church Music, Concordia University, Seward, NE, 28 July 2014), 11.

17. Eugene H. Peterson, *A Long Obedience in the Same Direction: Discipleship in an Instant Society* (InterVarsity Press, 1980), 185.

18. Since the psalms are prayers, they address our needs. For example, I like to use Psalm 37 in times of illness as words of encouragement. Words such as, "Be still before the Lord, and wait patiently for him … for the Lord loves the just and will not forsake his faithful ones" (37:7, 28 NIV) can be followed by, "Dear Lord, help Janet, who is struggling with illness today, to be confident that you will protect her and that you will never abandon her in her hour of need." Then, one could continue further into the psalm, read a little more, and then tailor another personal petition surrounding those words. I also like Psalm 139 in times of illness or distress as well. It speaks clearly that the Lord knows us and what we need. Psalm 128:1–4 works very well as a family blessing especially when a family receives the gift of a new child.

19. "Global E-mail Spam Rate from 2012 to 2018," Joseph Johnson, *Statista*, https://www.statista.com/statistics/270899/global-e-mail-spam-rate/. The rate in 2018 was 55%.

20. Oswald Chambers, *Workmen of God: The Cure of Souls* (Marshall, Morgan & Scott, 1937), 90.

21. Robert Butler, "The Life Review: An Interpretation of Reminiscence in the Aged," *Psychiatry* 26, no. 1 (1963): 65–76. In his groundbreaking work that paved the way for therapists and pastors to begin thinking about the possibilities surrounding self-narrative, Robert Butler mentions that older persons have shown it is a universal experience to engage in life review. Butler suggests that older persons find themselves reviewing life frequently and in ways almost beyond their control. The process of self-narrative, therefore, focuses the storyteller by adhering to specific life themes wherein pastors may discover pertinent spiritual needs.

22. See Charles V. Gerkin, *The Living Human Document: Re-Visioning Pastoral Counseling in a Hermeneutical Mode* (Abingdon, 1984), 112–17.

23. Senkbeil, *The Care of Souls*, 137.

24. "Understanding Grief and Loss: An Overview," *HealGrief*, https://healgrief.org/understanding-grief/?gclid=EAIaIQobChMI5ei42qb-7gIVGuy1Ch14YwaSEAAYASAAEgKk_PD_BwE.

25. "Journeying through Grief," *Stephen Ministries*, https://www.stephenministries.org/griefresources/default.cfm/774.

26. *Lutheran Service Book* (Concordia, 2006), 315.

27. See the prayers in the following: Lutheran Service Book, 305–18; Lutheran Service Book: Pastoral Care Companion; and The Book of

Common Prayer under the heading Prayers
and Thanksgivings. For the collects of the day,
see the Lutheran Service Book: Pastoral Care
Companion, 537–616, and The Book of Common
Prayer under the heading The Collects.

28. *Lutheran Worship: Altar Book* (Concordia, 1982),
141.

PASTORS CARE FOR A SOUL IN THE WAY A DOCTOR CARES FOR A BODY.

In a time when many churches have lost sight of the real purpose of the church, *The Care of Souls* invites a new generation of pastors to form the godly habits and practical wisdom needed to minister to the hearts and souls of those committed to their care.

"Pastoral theology at its best. Every pastor, and everyone who wants to be a pastor, should read this book."
—Timothy George, Founding Dean, Beeson Divinity School, Samford University; General Editor, Reformation Commentary on Scripture